In a world so broken by fatherlessness, Carlos' new book is a beacon of hope shining like a lighthouse. Many who are far from home will see the light in these pages and return to the heart of the Father.

JONATHAN DAVID HELSER
Recording Artist

Carlos is a strong, passionate man who has learnt what it means to be a son and a father to many around him. With piercing clarity he bravely shares his own journey towards the safety of embracing a life of spiritual sonship, amidst the sort of pride and pitfalls that we all face. This is a helpful wake-up call to our identity in Christ and also to being humble enough to realise that position isn't everything. Drawing extensively on the example of biblical characters in their own shaping and battles with identity, Carlos' work is beautifully and poetically written, yet disarmingly honest about the human condition. It will challenge you to answer his question "Whose son are you?" and it will propel you to live-out your inheritance of sonship to impact the world.

NICK ALLAN
Minister, St. Thomas' Philadelphia, Sheffield, United Kingdom

In the book "Simply Sonship" you will discover your greatest call to be a Son or Daughter of the King of Glory. While reading, I found myself laughing and crying as Carlos so elegantly revealed his personal journey of sonship. I would highly recommend this book because it serves as a road map of life, to break the orphan spirit and step into your birthright that Jesus purchased over 2000 years ago.

CHAD DEDMON
Pastor at Bethel Church

Carlos Rodriguez hits a homerun sharing his candid vulnerable journey of sonship.

PETER JACKSON
Itinerant Minister, Founder of Peter Jackson Ministries

Carlos and his wife Catherine are two of my favorite people on the planet. Just like the book of Hebrews describes how Jesus is the exact representation of the Father, these two represent the Father's heart with excellence. They do family so well, and God trusts them so much with His beloved family. Because their lives preach their message far more than any sermon ever could, I believe that this book is more than information, but more of an impartation to heal life's hurts. It invites you on a journey of sonship, and brings you into the most intimate relationship that you ever could have dreamed of with your Heavenly Father!!! Go on the journey of a lifetime into the very heart of your Heavenly Daddy. Bravo Carlos. Well done!!

SHARA PRADHAN
Director of Compelled By Love

As I began to read this book, my eyes began to flood at the acknowledgement of fathers. By the time I was five or six paragraphs in, little rivulets of water were pouring down my face. I had to set it down and try to compose myself. My heart was pounding and I was completely overcome. The Holy Spirit was soothing my aching heart and massaging my deepest fears.

It may have taken a year to write this book but it's taken 33 years to produce it. Carlos Rodriguez lives it. His life is the sermon, his surrender is the space between paragraphs, his example is an inspiration to a rock and roller like me. The lessons contained here are probably the hardest I've ever been faced with. But they are also the most liberating, the most freeing and the most yoke breaking joy of revelation I've ever heard. I owe that joy to Carlos Rodriguez and Simply Sonship.

If you are weighed down by perfectionism, competitiveness, insecurity and self-recrimination, you will find a key to that prison in the stories, anecdotes and revelations in this book. If you are struggling to understand the incredible grace extended by your Father; if you are desperate for examples on how to practically cultivate favour and opportunity; I believe the life lessons illustrated here will provide the answers you are searching for the way they have done for me.

BRIAN HOUSTON
Recording Artist

Reading the first chapter is like getting on a horse a little too wild to handle, but somehow the thrill is greater than the fear. Pastor Carlos has tapped into the untamed love of the Father and he is barely holding on. Rarely do I find a book well written by a man riding through life at full blast. Carlos takes us down the beaten path of the parable of the prodigal son and yet reveals to us unknown horizons of God's heart. Also, this book bleeds the sound theology of sonship which is so lacking in the church. It is a good read and a good jolt to the heart; in these pages we can hear the pounding thunder of Father running toward us.

PASTOR ANDREW MCMILLAN
Comunidad Cristiana de Fe, Medellin, Colombia

SIMPLY SONSHIP

A JOURNEY IN AUTHENTIC LOVE AND EXTRAVAGANT GRACE

CARLOS A. RODRIGUEZ

CATCH THE FIRE
BOOKS

Simply Sonship

Previously titled Designed For Inheritance (2014)

Published by Catch The Fire Books

272 Attwell Drive, Toronto ON M9W 6M3 Canada

Distributed worldwide by Catch The Fire Distribution. Titles may be purchased in bulk; for information, please contact distribution@catchthefire.com.

Catch The Fire® is a registered trademark of Catch The Fire World.

ISBN 978-1-894310-91-8

Copyright © 2016 Carlos A. Rodriguez

The Team:
Marcott Bernarde, Jo Dunbar, Hanna Glover, Benjamin Jackson, Jon Long, Steve Long, Rachel McDonagh, Jonathan Puddle, Miruna Veenhuis
Study Materials: Ally Proudfoot
Cover Design: Marcott Bernarde
Photography: Tonya Hurter
Interior layout: Medlar Publishing Solutions Pvt Ltd, India

Printed in Canada
First Edition (Designed For Inheritance) 2014
Second Edition 2016

Shelfie

A **free** eBook edition is available with the purchase of this print book.

CLEARLY PRINT YOUR NAME ABOVE IN UPPER CASE

Instructions to claim your free eBook edition:
1. Download the Shelfie app for Android or iOS
2. Write your name in **UPPER CASE** above
3. Use the Shelfie app to submit a photo
4. Download your eBook to any device

CONTENTS

Foreword 7

Dedication: To My Fathers 9

Introduction 11

1 One Father for All 13

2 The First Born 31

3 Daddy Issues 46

4 The Orphan Antidote 63

5 The Other "Father" 84

6 Really Good News 100

7 The Happy Number 2 116

8 Whose Son Are You? 129

9 Sonship to Your Own 143

10 The Pursuit 161

11 Original Imitation 177

12 A Fathered Generation 190

13 It's Your Turn! 200

Epilogue 215

Notes 217

Acknowledgments 223

About the Author 225

FOREWORD

Every now and then a new book is released that literally causes an explosion in my heart and presses the reset button in the very core of my being. This is one of those books and I love it, just as I love the author, Carlos Rodriguez, my best friend, colleague and son in Christ Jesus.

This book is infused with God. It is brilliantly written, intertwining biblical revelation, dynamic insights, and gripping, real life stories straight from the heart of a truly great son of God. Carlos, humbly, yet powerfully manifests his unshakeable identity in the Father, whilst inviting us all beautifully into this glorious sonship that can be ours through faith in Jesus Christ the Son of God. Carlos, a true father, does this in such a way that leaves me fully convinced that as you read this book, you will, like me, be drawn into a deeply powerful encounter through tears and laughter, with the great God of love Himself, and you will never be the same again. This book is a must read that will leave you marked forever. You too will begin to manifest the greatness of your sonship, living an extraordinary, supernatural life that only God can live, passionately giving away your infinite inheritance in extreme generosity to a broken, orphaned world longing to come home to the Father.

Duncan Smith
President of Catch The Fire World
Author of *Consumed By Love*

TO MY FATHERS

Carlos Alberto Rodríguez Ortíz (Papi) who gave himself for us everyday, and is my greatest example to follow. Te amo mi viejo.

John Arnott who took me in as his intern at 19, ordained me to the ministry at 23 and still makes room for me at 34. Gracias amigo.

Duncan Smith who continues to challenge me, believe in me and share his victories with me. I imitate you, as you imitate Christ.

Abba, who chose me before I chose Him, who trusted me with my wife and kids and who never stops surprising me with goodness. Your knee will always be my home. I love you.

INTRODUCTION

I owe an explanation to my wife. And, I owe an explanation to all the other wives, sisters, mothers, daughters and women who read these lines today. This is a book on sonship. The term "son" normally implies husband, brother, father, boy, male.

But according to Scripture, "In Christ Jesus you are all sons of God, through faith. For as many of you as were baptized into Christ have put on Christ. There is neither Jew nor Greek, there is neither slave nor free, there is no male and female, for you are all one in Christ Jesus." [1]

My desire is to invite all of us to walk in the full benefits of sonship. For us to know and embrace the joy of being God's favorite son. You ladies are God's sons, just as we guys—for all of eternity—will be the bride of Christ.

Thank you Jack Frost for giving your life to share this message. We will see you at the wedding, dressed in white.

CHAPTER ONE

ONE FATHER FOR ALL

What comes into our minds when we think about God
is the most important thing about us. — AW TOZER

I can still feel the adrenaline and hope that rushed through me that spring morning in 2007. I was invited to speak at one of the biggest public schools in Puerto Rico; to a classroom filled with the most "discipline-challenged" students that could be gathered. Pregnant teenagers, young addicts and detention experts, all forced to listen to my sermon for thirty minutes.

"Finally, a chance to see if this message I kept preaching worked outside the church walls!"—at least, that was the mindset that drove me to accept the invitation. Then, in order to achieve my hyper religious expectations, I felt a need to be extra spiritual:

Increase the use of my divine gifts? *Check* ✔

Add some extra verses to my Bible reading? *Check* ✔
Use Hebrew words in all my prayers? *Check* ✔
Extend my worship times? *Check* ✔
Do minimal amounts of sin? ... *Almost checked*

The chosen Friday arrived and I remember walking the hallways on my way to the classroom with prayer-warrior-intercession-of-the-angelic-kind under my breath, and the list of won battles in my pocket. As I stepped past the door, I noticed four teachers who stood quietly in a corner. They gave me a short glance and looked at each other with eyes rolled in skepticism. It took me ten seconds to understand why.

The room was stuffed with eighty, loud and careless souls. There were young couples that manifested their love publicly with no shame and extravagant affection. Some students had gold chains around their necks that could have paid my mortgage. Others looked angry with the world, and especially with me. My holy confidence diminished with every step I took amongst the mass of rowdy high school students. The scene instantly took me back to the years when I would have to deal with popular guys, determined bullies and teenage love rejections. In a moment, all the self-won anointing abandoned me. I forgot my opening jokes and the Bible verses I had planned to preach from. Cold sweat overtook my body and I knew that I looked nervous and lost (because I was so nervous and so lost).

Suddenly, like a warm fire on a cold winter night, a picture flickered in my mind: Carol Arnott stepping back into her Father's embrace.

In my time of interning for the Arnotts, I heard her explain: "Whenever I feel fearful or insecure in front of people, all I have to do is remember God's presence. Then, I take a step back into the arms of the Father and receive a hug from the one who is always standing right behind me."

It had been more than four years since I left Catch The Fire Toronto but in that moment of great distress, while the teachers were trying to get control of the crowd, I remembered Mama Carol. Then, I turned my back to the students, faced the whiteboard in front of the room and closed my eyes. I took a step back with my shaking knees into my Father's embrace and instantly felt His company. Immediately, I heard a known whisper: "Carlos, they don't need a prepared sermon, they need a prepared life, and you my son, are prepared." Without analyzing His words, I believed in my heart, took a deep breath and everything changed.

As the director of the school finished the introduction, I turned to faced the prodigals in front of me and began to share from Luke 15. Suddenly, I remembered the jokes, delivered them famously and the group responded with laughter.

Make them smile? *Check* ✔

I was then animated and entertaining while sharing the story of the prodigal son.

Keep their attention? *Check* ✔

I was also vulnerable and open while forgetting my religious efforts.

Remember His unconditional love? *Double check* ✔✔

Here I was in a public school, able to share one of the most powerful illustrations in all of scripture; a son who goes to his father to request the share of his inheritance, as if to wish him dead. The father in the story responds not by putting up a fight, but rather by sharing his life and wealth. The younger son goes away fully loaded, far away from home to foreign lands. He wastes his inheritance on food, gambling, paid sex and other temporary pleasures. Almost finding true happiness. But as the money runs out, hunger strikes. Now, the boy who lacked nothing becomes a beggar, willing to eat pigs' leftovers.

From the students' reaction, I could tell that some had already heard the story, while others had no clue where this was going. Twenty minutes into it, I called out to an uninterested young man in the back. "Can you help me act out the climactic scene of the son's return?" I asked. Everyone started laughing while explaining to me his usual unwillingness. Hence, I pushed a little more and like a miracle to all his friends, he agreed.

"Sure, I'll help. Sleeping around and wasting money on drinking and gambling … Easy for me to act this guy out," said the young man confidently. To my joy he got into full character; acted like a drunk, pretended to kiss the girls around him, and walked slowly to the back corner. He was perfect.

Meanwhile, I read out loud from Luke 15:17-20, "When the son came to his senses, he said, 'How many of my father's hired servants have food to spare, and here I am starving to death! I will set out and go back to my father and say to him: Father, I have sinned against heaven and against you. I am no longer worthy to be called your son; make me like one of your hired servants.' So, he got up and went to his father." I went to the furthest spot of the room and invited my willing actor to repeat the words that the prodigal son said. Silence began to creep in as he cleared his throat and quoted, "Father, I have sinned against heaven and against you. I am no longer worthy to be called your son." With more than half of the class sitting in between us, I asked him to repeat those words and walk with his head low, towards me. As he did, I took a step back and said, "When the son decided to go back home, this is how the Father reacted." Then I smiled, opened my arms and started running violently across the room.

As I crashed with the prodigal son in front of me, I began to kiss him on our way to the floor. The room went from extreme laughter to quiet shock when I yelled at the top of my lungs: "This is how the Father reacts to you!"

More than half of them, including the boy who acted as the prodigal son began to cry. I repeated, "Daddy God loves your homecoming!" "Daddy God loves your homecoming!" while I continued to kiss him, hug him and look into as many eyes as I could catch.

After letting go of my crying actor, I started to embrace others and they began to fall to the floor, broken by God's evident grace. I watched as fellow students reached out to each other and began to ask for forgiveness. Strong men were on their knees repenting and young women lifted their hands in surrender to God.

Meanwhile, my friend Carli, who had been given another group of younger students to share with, walked into the classroom, looked at me in awe and began to worship with his guitar. We led them through prayers of forgiveness and welcoming. As the kids continued to line up for prayer, the skeptics were now teary-eyed believers who hugged and prayed with their most difficult students.

That morning, I stood in the middle of the greatest revival meeting I had ever attended. God manifested His love in this glorious chaos and

I witnessed the healing of multiple hearts. Heaven came to earth, sons and daughters met their true Father, grace was evident and touchable, and my life has never been the same.

Standing before this live scene of the gospel I began to understand something that seemed really obvious to Jesus: The world is desperate for a loving father. Jesus knows this loving Father intimately and eternally. And His greatest joy was to share Him with us all. Happy sonship to all!

And good news, the message remains the same. No matter where you have been in life, or what you have been involved in, the Father is willing to change it all. He's the Daddy every person needs to come home to.

The Prodigal Father

Jesus used Luke 15 to expose the three conditions of the human soul. The audience who listened were sinners who wanted to be near Him and the religious leaders who criticized His approachability. He took advantage of this mixed crowd and used stories that were easy to relate to. His intention with each parable was to express God's desire to find the lost.

The first story is about a lost sheep. The shepherd leads the search for the sheep who does not know how to return home. When the good shepherd finds the lost sheep, He carries it on his shoulders, rejoicing. He's happy with the rescue, not disappointed at the loss. This narrates the work of Jesus, who always leaves the 99 behind in order to find "the one."

The second parable is about a lost coin. The owner puts all of her efforts in the search, for the coin itself does not know it needs to be found. This story relates to the work of the Holy Spirit to convict sinners of their sin. It speaks of mercy and celebration as the valuable treasure returns to its rightful owner. And there is joy before the angels.

The third and last parable is about the lost son. The prodigal who knew his father, left him behind but later chooses to return.

The highlight of each story is about the joy experienced when the lost return home. It's the *manifesto* of the New Covenant: Jesus will rescue the sheep, Holy Spirit will convict the sinner and Father will welcome the sons.

These stories also speak of affection demonstrated. Jesus is not just giving us the information, "God is love"; He is teaching in words and action how He actually loves. In the third parable especially, He uses verbs to show us the actions of the Father's love; "But while he (the younger son) was still a long way off, his father *saw* him and was *filled* with compassion for him; he *ran* to his son, *threw* his arms around him and *kissed* him." [1]

During the first century, a patriarch man never ran. If he were to run, he would have to hitch up his tunic so he would not trip. If he did this, his legs would be exposed which constitutes an act of indignity based on the tradition of the time.

However, the father reacted with great excitement at the sight of his son and saved him from *kezazah*; a ceremony where the community would break a large pot in front of the now Gentile son and yell, "You are cut off from your people!" So the father ran and humiliated himself to get to his son before his law-abiding neighbors. The village would have followed the father and witnessed their embrace as he fell upon his neck and kissed his son fervently and repeatedly. After this emotional reunion, it was clear that there would be no gathering for *kezazah* and there would be no rejecting this son—despite what he had done.

The father's reaction is what we know as redemption. He expresses love even as he ignores the religious prayer of repentance. He gives no acknowledgement to the words and prayer his son rehearsed on the journey back. If he would have acknowledged those prayers then the son would have believed the lie, "He welcomes me back because I was willing to be a servant." In everyone's eyes, being a servant would have been a just and fair treatment, but the father had enough servants, what he wanted was his boy. Instead of paying attention to his son's "repentance" the father called out to his actual servants to bring the best robe, one reserved only for the father, and only for the most special of occasions. Once again, he got his child to look like him and declared, by putting shoes on his feet, that he walked as an owner on the property. There were no more rocks to hurt the young man's feet, no more heat to burn his skin, every step from that moment onwards would feel like forgiveness. Then the father gave his son a ring, just like Pharaoh did when he removed his signet ring and put it on Joseph's hand as he was installed into office in Egypt. [2] The ring carried the family seal and from that moment onwards his inheritance was returned. Wherever the son would press his finger on a wax receipt, the price for anything was paid in full. This lost child now looked like his father, walked like his father and could rule like his father. The boy became a vessel for prodigal grace.

Even if the story stopped there, it would have been offensive enough, challenging enough and glorious enough. But, like a man drunk with joy, the father puts no limit to the occasion. He continued his display of extravagance with a party: "Bring the fattened calf and kill it, and let us eat and celebrate," [3] exclaimed the father between smiles, hugs and tears of joy. There were zero accomplishments to highlight, no degrees earned, no sports game won, this party was purely based on unconditional love. This happy dad was willing to show off his mercy and celebrate the fact that his boy was alive. And everyone was invited to taste and see, that this father was good.

The word "prodigal" means "recklessly extravagant, having spent everything, given in abundance, lavish." [4] Jesus was not trying to define the quality of the sinner in the parable; He was exposing the character of His Father. The message conveyed was this; it is not about what we do right or wrong, but about how *right* He loves us, even when we do wrong. God the Father is the true prodigal in this story and the true prodigal for every son and daughter.

With you He is recklessly extravagant, having spent everything, given in abundance, and oh so lavish.

There is a desperate need for our generation to meet this happy Father—both in the body of Christ and outside of it. And although this parable is commonly used to invite "backsliders" to come back home, the "prodigal son behavior" is inside most of us. At church, we live in the Father's house but we are more interested in His inheritance than His person. We want the anointing for ministry, revelation to prepare a sermon, ideas so we can make money. Then we go to the foreign lands of ambition, spend it all on ourselves and when hunger strikes, we repent. We return with a pay-him-back mentality willing to be hired servants. Yet God is interested in our closeness to Him, not in the amount of our religious repentance or the quality of our efforts and service.

The irrational parable finishes with another encounter, one that unfortunately is also familiar in the modern church. The elder son, who was working in the field, reproaches the father's wastefulness and calls out the sins of his brother. In doing so, he exposes his own jealousy and judgments. As a man consumed with work, the older brother could not accept this irrational celebration. To him, the wrong message was being sent and the father was giving the stamp of approval to his brother's rebellion. In his eyes, the right thing was for his dad to correct his baby brother and in turn, acknowledge the value of *his* service and faithfulness.

Yet the father's response was true for him, and for all of us: "You are always with me and all that I have is yours." This statement reveals the love of God for all his children; those who leave home in rebellion and the ones who stay home feeling rejected. This is a father that truly knows how to define a child, and to such a father, we all want to belong.

All you have to do is say *yes*. Whether you are lost like the sheep and can't find your way back, whether you are lost like the coin and have no clue, or, as the younger son, you are lost and you know where you belong, the Prodigal Father wants you to return so He can run to your encounter. This is the sermon Jesus preached. This is the life He manifested. This is the story that will save the world.

The Son's Mission

The son of God became the son of man, so that the
sons of men could become the sons of God.
— ST IRENAEUS

Jesus left everything that made Him God, adopted human form and came to earth to be a servant of all. What never changed in this epic journey, was His identity as son. The main role of the son Jesus was to reveal the Father He has known for eternity. He did not come to "free" himself from his Father's rule, but rather to establish that rule through a life surrendered in obedience and love.

The ancient Israelites knew God through a series of descriptive names: Creator, *Yahweh*, God of the Angel Armies, The Great I Am, and the list goes on. Each name carries part of God's identity; an expression of the many ways He had related to His people until that moment. However, the name for God in the New Testament is Father, the holiest name you will ever hear. And His Son came to teach us how to call Him by this new first name: *Abba*. Not new because He recently became *Abba* Father, but new as when you see an old friend in a new light (and maybe you fall in love).

Therefore, when the disciples wanted to learn how to pray, Jesus shared with them, "Our Father in Heaven" a statement that, up to that moment, had only belonged to Him. Father was also the name Jesus used every time He referred to God, with only one exception. At the cross, when the Son took upon himself separation from His Father and cried out a portion of Psalm 22: "My God, my God, why have you forsaken me?" It is because of this moment of separation between the Father and His Son, that we can now be connected eternally to this Trinitarian Love.

We can now, always, confidently say, "My Father, My Father, You are always with me."

Jesus died because He had a Father too extraordinary to keep for Himself, and His death was the only vehicle that could provide our reunion.

We are now able to respond to the Father who runs, kisses, hugs, ignores religion and puts His best garments on us. He is the one who will never deny us the return of our inheritance. So the party in heaven has been pre-planned for whenever you decide to come home.

Your acceptance, your belonging, and your sonship were always the plan; "For he chose us in Him before the creation of the world to be holy and blameless in His sight. **In love He predestined us for adoption to sonship** through Jesus Christ, in accordance with his pleasure and will." [5]

God has forever been a Father and that's the way He has chosen to identify Himself with. Not just with us, but with everyone who is His creation and workmanship, even those that don't believe. The apostle Paul shared this revelation with the pagans of Athens, "For, in him we live and move and have our being, or as some of your own poets have said, 'We are his offspring.'" [6]

To unbelievers and to us, God is the beginning and the end. We were all made by Him and for Him, with no choice in the matter. We are offspring by creation, handmade by an artist of love and alive because of His breath in our lungs. Yet Jesus made a way for the ones who were created to choose whether or not they want relationship with the Creator; a father-son relationship with the one who is Love. God's choice was to predetermine us for sonship through adoption. Our choice is whether we stay in the orphanage of sin, or come home to His festival of hope.

The Father Who Gives Identity

Jesus is God the Son but He lived life as the Son of God. He embraced sonship, and sonship is a glorious captivity. In it, you will always be the "son of"; there will always be authority over you. And there is a powerful freedom available for those willing to live under this custody. Jesus chose to live confined to His sonship, not because of weakness, but because He knew who He was, and how much He was loved.

Besides, it is inevitable that children emulate their fathers. The normal thing is for a child to act and talk like his father (and it's always adorable). When the son's identity becomes a reflection of a father's character without diminishing his own name, he is expressing sonship to the fullest, as Jesus did with God. "He only did what He saw His Father doing and only said what He heard His Father saying."[7] God and Jesus modeled perfect oneness. But Jesus who was confined in love, not only worked in His heavenly Father's business, He also carried the identity as the carpenter's son.[8] The Son of God with all intents and purposes also became the son of a man. Both His heavenly Father and His earthly adopted father had a rightful place to define Him.

The word father is described as "the one who gives identity to his children." It is the nature of a father figure to define, to give a name, to influence and shape. No matter how hard we try, the dads in our lives will be there with full rights to determine who we are. For better or for worse, either present or while absent, fathers shape the identity inside us all. Although we have the benefit of a perfect Father God, we also carry the burden of having imperfect males as His representation on earth.

People around us are able to interact with our earthly father through us. When they see us, they meet with our dad. If not in our gestures, it will be in our political views, our mellow personality or explosive anger, spirituality or indifference, achievements or disappointments, our funny noses or weird shaped heads. In a way, our father is always around, and we can either repel him or accept him. We can either recognize that connection or deny it forever.

Most of us would agree that a good dad is caring, loving and affirming, willing to guide, correct, motivate, coach and encourage. The ideal father would be someone with a steady presence, a constant voice, the provider who can also spend time being silly with his kids. But dads are not perfect. The identity that these earthly men are able to provide is always broken; there will always be a gap, something will be missing (I know this as a son, and as a dad.)

Some of us have experienced physical abuse through them and the image of a father awakens feelings of hate, fear and loss, thus we identify ourselves as victims. Others never met the guy and feel continually abandoned. Or perhaps we are not even looking for any father figure because we hated our dads and want nothing to do with him, so we develop an orphan identity. We work so hard not to be like our father only to realize that's the same thing our fathers did.

The fact is that we are all wearing lenses that distort the view of the world around us. These glasses have the prescription of the experiences we've had with our parental figures. The way we see life is primarily shaped by the words our parents have spoken over us. Even our image of God and our hope to be welcomed into any relationship, is influenced by the kind of approval we received in our natural family.

If your biological father is not in your heart as a true father, he will be in your soul as bitterness and that pain will either be transformed or transmitted. We can change it into something beautiful or we will share it with others as anger, shame or fear.

You and I are like the kids in that high school. We have a desperate need for the Father that Jesus already revealed. We carry a wound inflicted by the fathers in our lives and only the heavenly Father can heal that disease. Yes, we can learn many things without these fathers, but our hearts will always yearn for a prodigal Father to receive us. We can try to drown out the request of our soul with apparent success, but we will never escape the fact that we were created to be children who belong. This book is an invitation for us all to be Sons of God *and* to be Sons of Men. To understand that the definition of "me" can only be found in God the Father and once that is properly defined, we can truly be sons and daughters to others; and then become fathers and mothers ourselves.

In the beginning of it all, Father, Son and Holy Spirit created us by saying, "Let us make man in our own image and likeness." Why not embrace the truth that you were formed on the inside of a Father who loved His Son and who is Spirit—just like you. Your DNA carries the code of *Abba* and all that is required is for you to receive what already belongs to you since aeons past.

For most of my life I have struggled to find God, to know God, to love God. I have tried hard to follow the guidelines of the spiritual life—pray always, work for others, read the Scriptures—and to avoid the many temptations to dissipate myself. I have failed many times but always tried again, even when I was close to despair. All this time God has been trying to find me, to know me, and to love me. The question is not "How am I to find God?" but "How am I to let myself be found by him?" The question is not "How am I to know God?" but "How am I to let myself be known by God?" And, finally, the question is not "How am I to love God?" but "How am I to let myself be loved by God?"

The great theologian Henri Nouwen asked these questions and came across the right answers. His conclusions did not come when he corrected his theology or went to the right meetings. Nouwen did not find solutions through someone else's experience. Faced with the painting of the prodigal son's return, Nouwen discovered that His answer was the Father Himself; revealed and manifested as the father in Luke 15. This Father, who is God and who is love, is the one whose eternal desire was for you to be adopted as His beloved. He is lovely in every way, merciful to the reckless, sweet to the hurting and available to us—the broken. The most loving and caring God is above everything else, your Dad.

If we stopped for a moment to see Him, not through our pain, our rejection or our religion, we might discover that He is everything we will ever need. Without fear, we can return from foreign lands and encounter the Prodigal Father who will receive us and embrace us forever. He wants to transform how we define the word "Father" and He is able to properly define who we are in Him. He is the One you are yearning for and this is the relationship that is available for you.

Now, the basic requirement is for you to believe in the answer to this one simple question: Am I loved perfectly by the extravagant Father?

Absolutely ... *Check* ✔

STUDY GUIDE: CHAPTER 1
ONE FATHER FOR ALL

The Prodigal Father story is taken from Luke 15.
Read all of Luke 15 now.

Which of the sons in the story do you most identify with?
The younger son who knows where he belongs but turned his back on his father, or the elder son who has always been in the father's house but is full of envy and jealousy. In what ways does this manifest itself in your life through your beliefs and/or behaviour?

> *"God's choice was to predetermine us for sonship through adoption. Our choice is whether we remain as orphans in a dying world or live in His family today."*

Are you able to say yes to living in God's family as a son or daughter? If not, what holds you back?
The role of a father is to give identity.

> *"The fact is that we are all wearing lenses that distort the view of the world around us. These glasses have the prescription of the experiences we've had with our parental figures...."*

What prescription is in your lenses? What are your experiences of your earthly father? Are you able to identify how this lens has affected the way you view your Heavenly Father?

Carlos sites a quote by Henri Nouwen, which contains the following questions:

1. How am I to let myself be found by God?
2. How am I to let myself be known by God?
3. How am I to let myself be loved by God?
4. How would you answer each of these questions?

The answer to these questions may be found in identifying the behaviours or beliefs that you have which have built a barrier to you being found, known and loved. Taking down these barriers is the first step in answering these questions.

CHAPTER TWO

THE FIRST BORN

Jesus is what God has to say.

— BRIAN ZAHND

It is ridiculous to try to tackle the sonship of Jesus in one chapter. We are talking about the longest, healthiest and most fruitful relationship in all of history. Before there ever was any other concept there has always been the family of God; Father, Son and Holy Spirit. St. Francis of Assisi explained it like this, "God has been the Father eternally loving the son, Jesus has been the son who has reciprocated that love perfectly, and the Holy Spirit has been the love that flows continually between them."

Before John called Jesus "The Word" His Father called Him "Son." Before His disciples called Him "Teacher" His Father called Him "Son." Before the Pharisees called Him a "Drunk" His Father called Him "Son." And before any of us could ever call Him: "Lord, God,

Lion, Lamb, Master, Savior, Teacher, Lover, Shepherd, King, Christ or Friend," His Father has always called Him, "Son."

The Father defines, the Son receives, the Spirit empowers. No better connection has ever been seen. No other community could ever compare. No greater relationship will ever exist.

And relationship is very different from religion. Yet according to estimates, there are roughly 4,200 religions in the world. That's four thousand two hundred ways, to try and fail. Each one of these religions is the result of hundreds of years of man- made-effort, deviated revelations and self-righteous glorification. It is the same pursuit that brought divided tongues upon those working at the tower of Babel after they said in one voice, "Let us build ourselves a city, with a tower that reaches to the heavens, so that we may make a name for ourselves."[1] The beginning of religion is here: let us work, let us get to heaven, let us find identity.

In His kindness God gave the law to Moses to prove that we could never work hard enough to earn His kindness; that humans can never gain the heaven we pursue, because ultimately, we don't even know who we are. All those complicated parameters in the book of Leviticus remind us repeatedly that we need a Savior who can complete the work, a Messiah to come from heaven, a champion to bring us into true identity. This Godly religious law proves that we need God (Jesus) to find God (Father) by the power of God (the Holy Spirit). The deeper we go into the Trinity, the more we will realize how needy we are, and the more dependent we will become.

Therefore, the Son of God did not descend from eternity to begin a religion; He came to show us the way to the Father. His mission and vision was not to write a new manual of rules and regulations. He did not give up His life to ensure you make it to church on Sundays. He lived a perfect life so that you could receive perfect love from Monday through Saturday (and then celebrate it together with your church family). The love which was always available, even before the Law.

It only takes a read through the gospels, wearing the right glasses, to see sonship in everything Jesus did. To be exposed to the depth of the relationship that the Son had with the Father. To learn from the man who fulfilled the requirements of religion so that we could be filled with the glory of His intimacy.

There is a progression in the book of Mark that reveals the journey of the Son, Jesus, during His time on earth. The progression goes like this: *He is loved, He is promoted, He surrenders.* It is possible that this march will be duplicated in your life. I hope it is. And if it is, well, you're in good company.

He is Loved

At last He is surrounded by water. Above Him the heavens are ripped apart with excitement. It is the day of His baptism and while John stands in awe of this holy moment, the Spirit descends on Jesus like a dove. While His long hair drips with muddy water, a voice from above is heard saying, "You are My beloved Son, in whom I am well pleased." [2] As Brennan Manning has said, "What an earthquake in the human soul of Jesus!" [3] An open vision followed by impartation from the Spirit and the voice of the Father affirming His heart. The love of the Trinity perfectly exposed in a happy family encounter.

This day has been thirty years in the making. Jesus the carpenter was about to do the work of Jesus the Christ. After this simple act of baptism Jesus would begin His active work of the ministry. This seems like the perfect opportunity to make a grand introduction of the Messiah who would save Israel. The Father could have used His booming voice to say the statements that would establish the validity of Jesus in front of the multitude. But He finds nothing more important to say than: "I love you Son, I'm proud of you." It's all about definition.

In this spiritual immersion of holy love, the man Jesus comes out of the waters symbolically covered in our sin and filth. He has no legalistic reason to be baptized. Baptism was for the forgiveness of sin and He is the one person who can legitimately say: "I have never sinned!"

Jesus should not have responded to John's invitation of repentance. It is actually problematic for His reputation. Staying pure, holy and blameless was the requirement for His sacrifice at the cross to be valid. He is giving the critics the perfect excuse to challenge His integrity and it seems like John the Baptist knows this. He says to Jesus, "I need to be baptized by you!" Yet Jesus wants to fulfill **all** righteousness (His, yours and mine). The only reason for being immersed in the River Jordan was to be fully immersed in you and me. He cared more about being obedient to the Father than about what others could say later.

"Therefore he had to be made like His brothers in every respect." [4] Just like us, fully human in every way.

Jesus has to enter into the drama of human existence
for that belongs to the core of His mission.

— POPE BENEDICT XVI [5]

Here in the beginning of His life in ministry, He proclaims this truth through His actions: "I'm not doing these 33 years as me, I'm doing them as you!" He started off the transformation of the world around Him not by a confirmation of how much He was God, but by affirming how much He was like us.

If Jesus made our moment of repentance His moment of obedience, then this moment of acceptance belongs to us. Author Ed Piorek likes to call these verses in Mark, the *Central Event.* "The heavens are torn open. The Holy Spirit descends on you like a dove and a voice from above is heard saying, 'You, [insert your name here] are my beloved son/daughter, in you I am well pleased.'"

There is no mention in the New Testament of any catastrophic event where the heavens were stitched back together. Because you are a son in the First Born, you walk under an open heaven. Always. You will find no verses that tells us of the horrible day when the Holy Spirit stopped descending; quite the opposite, you have become His temple and He still comes upon you as fire. There is also no theology anywhere from Mark 1:11 to Revelation 22:20 that would suggest that God is not a Father anymore. Confirmed in multiple occasions is the truth that you are still His beloved, and He is still pleased with you. This is available, every moment of every day, because the only begotten Son became the firstborn of many. [6] Jesus walked in perfect obedience to God His Father as if you and I had walked in perfect obedience to God our Father. His life was to our credit and it is now on *our* account.

He is the only begotten Son, and now the first begotten Son by resurrection. Thanks to Christ we are the children of God and that story, introduced in the gospel of Mark, can be our daily reality if we believe. For "he who is joined to the Lord becomes **one** spirit with Him." [7]

He is Promoted

Fast forward to Mark chapter 9 and the son Jesus is now known as the Miracle-Maker-Prophet-Rabbi who feeds the people fish and heavenly words. It has been a while since His baptism and by this point in the story the disciples have been chosen, multitudes have been healed, and a whole nation feels the rumblings of change. In verse two Jesus is with three of His closest friends: Peter, James and John. They get front row seats to what the early church fathers called *The Transfiguration*. In all His splendor, Jesus is metamorphosed before them. They can barely see His skin, they mostly see glory and light. Somehow they recognize that Moses and Elijah appear next to Jesus and they begin to talk. Then, "A cloud appeared and covered them, and a voice came from the cloud: 'This is my Son, whom I love. Listen to him!'" [8]

Glorious. Jesus went from seeing the heavens open in Mark 1 to being surrounded by heaven in Mark 9. And again, there comes that statement that confirms His ultimate identity: "This is my Son, I love Him." Yet another Central Event.

It was Moses and Elijah who were talking to Jesus when the Father makes the statement: "Listen to Him!" Note that the exclamation point after "Listen to Him!" was not added by me for emphasis. The voice of the Father is heard aloud and with authority as He invites those around Him to pay attention to the message Jesus was sharing. Moses was there as the man who represents the Law. Elijah was there as the man who represents the prophets. Jesus stands between them as the one who represents the simple, happy news of sonship.

You can imagine the Father pointing to His Son as He looks at

Him with eyes of love, a smile on His face and says, "Listen to Him!" In other words, You have memorized the Law and it was good, but now listen to grace. You heard the warnings of the prophets and they were good, now listen to hope.

Listen to His voice when he forgives the adulterous woman. Listen to His rebuke of the Pharisees religion. Listen to Him as He declares healing to the lepers. Listen to His voice as He prays in the distance. Listen to Him as He preaches about the Kingdom. Listen to Him as He shares everything with His disciples.

Hear the rhythm of heaven as you receive the gift you never deserved; the unmerited favor in aggressive forgiveness. Watch as He grabs your sin and throws it to the depths of the ocean. See, as He cancels your debt of eternal damnation and offers the gift of eternal life. Grace, grace, grace.

"Listen to Him!" is a verbal statement from God that speaks of approval. It is a declaration of promotion to the things that were coming. At His baptism the Father's love spoke to Jesus without any expectation, "I love you, I'm pleased with you." The words were said before any miracles were performed or any parables preached, thus revealing the nature of the Father: He loves because *He* does, not because *we* do.

But this second time as the Son is transfigured, the voice says, "I love my Son, now listen to Him!" Jesus was loved by the Father not because of the miracles, or the sermons or the willingness to suffer at the cross. He was loved first and foremost because He is the Son. Jesus as a man responded to that love by being obedient to death. And so the progression goes: He is loved independently of His doing *and* He is promoted because He obeys. True sonship always finds a way to respond.

He Surrenders

Now in Mark 14, we hear a different voice. There is no Holy Spirit being manifested. This time it is not the Father who is speaking out of the clouds. We stand next to Jesus in the darkest night of His life, and a sense of dread surrounds Him. He tells His disciples in the garden of Gethsemane that the sorrow feels like death. It is this broken, quivery voice that we hear in prayer. "Going a little farther, he fell to the ground and prayed that if possible the hour might pass from him. 'Abba Father,' he said, 'everything is possible for you. Take this cup from me. Yet not what I will, but what you will.'" [9]

The Son of God is at breaking point. Most sons and daughters alive, in one way or another, have experienced this. You feel like it is impossible to go on. What comes upon you feels so heavy and so surreal. Thoughts are erratic, emotions are high, and you feel out of control. Jesus knows what that's like.

The holy man who has never sinned has an opportunity here. He can decide to take a different road than the one the Father had set for Him. And the full measure of His humanity is expressed when He claims to have a will that is different from the will of God. From this it becomes clear that His ability to stay pure, to heal the lame and to stop the storm was not based on His "God-ness" but on His surrender as a son. He came as a servant who was full of the Spirit, and that made all the difference. He stood and acted on this one truth, "The Father loves the Son and shows him all he does." [10] And He did it all by choice. The obedience Jesus manifested was not pre-downloaded into Him at conception; it was learned through experience and lived out in faith.

He had to decide on a daily basis to do the Father's will: He could have always said *no* but He determined to always say *yes*.

And here is the hardest *yes* any human has had to face. Knowing what was coming, Jesus asks for a different way, a different cup to drink. He saw himself at the cross, naked, beaten and bruised and pleaded for something else, anything else.

> *The most astounding thing about Jesus is that he is brutally honest*
> *about his feelings yet absolutely submitted to the will of God.*
>
> — TIMOTHY KELLER [11]

It is in this moment of decision where the Lord God is called *Abba* for the first time ever. No one before had considered using that word to address God. This was understood to be too familiar, not reverent enough. Yes, there are revelations in the Old Testament about his fatherly ways but actually calling Him *Abba*? "Daddy?" Never. No one.

But here is Jesus the Son, in His greatest night of weakness, calling out to His Papa the Strong. It is the sound of an infant who knows no other way to endure, but to ask *Abba* to come help him. In the presence of the cup of wrath, Jesus encounters comfort from His Father. This was absolute brokenness reaching out to absolute wholeness. And we were all in Jesus at that moment. We were all calling out to Daddy God. We all made the right choice in Him: "Yet not what I will, but what you will." [12]

This prayer of surrender happened more than once for "again he went away and prayed, saying the same words." [13] Jesus had to go back to *Abba* and continue to declare His obedience. Drenched in sweat and blood, His soul required continual acceptance of this yielding. He who was baptized into our humanity is now making the ultimate human choice.

> *It is in this valley of decision where the white flag of surrender becomes the tent we make our homes in.* — ASH SMITH

In His submission to our humanity, Jesus was able to exercise the gift of free will. The difference is, with that gift, He decided to do "the Father's will" in all situations. Surrendered as a son, Jesus set aside His own desires.

In this simple prayer, Jesus dies to the inclination of every man to go his own way. In this difficult prayer the son Jesus decides on true sonship. In this perfect prayer, a heart surrendered to God was fully manifested. And it became the best thing *we* have ever done.

The gospel is not "*What would Jesus do?*" but rather "*What Jesus did already!*" It is impossible for us to live the life that God the Father deserves. The demand of His irrefutable perfection is zero errors on all fronts. This is unreachable and unattainable for sinners. It was Christ who chose to obey God and it was He who lived the required life.

It is possible for us now to trust the Father in our times of suffering, transition and decision. Jesus made a way for us now to be the ones who pray: "Not my will, but yours!"

"For if we have been *united with him* in a death like his, we shall certainly be *united with him* in a resurrection like his. We know that our old self was *crucified with him* in order that the body of sin might be brought to nothing, so that we would no longer be enslaved to sin.

For one who has died has been set free from sin. Now if we have died with Christ, *we believe that we will also live with him.*" [14]

Onwards the Savior went to calvary, fully satisfying the justice of God. His service and obedience the best example of sonship. He was spat on by His leaders, beaten by His enemies and denied by His friends. Jesus died the death of a sinner, but rose again three days later as our champion liberator. Now, we are forever God's lovely ones, orphans no more.

Abba is now and eternally your Father. Jesus is now and eternally one with you. The relationship they have eternally enjoyed now belongs to you by the Holy Spirit. You have been adopted into the full rights of the firstborn. And no matter the names that you have been called in the past by fathers and mothers and teachers and lovers, you are not a "sinner" or a "dumbass" or a "jerk." God the Father will always call *you* "Son."

But, how do you act when life is out of your control? How do you react when things are not going your way? Can you truly see God as your Abba when pain is all around you? The answer to these questions are linked to the answer to this one: have you ever experienced the Central Event?

It takes the faith of a child to see in the Spirit what belongs to you because of resurrection. So this again is for you: "The heavens are torn open. The Holy Spirit descends on you like a dove and a voice from above is heard saying, 'You, [insert your name here] are my beloved son/daughter, in you I am well pleased.'"

Read it out aloud a couple of times and let it sink into your heart. Recognize the voice of *Abba* Father as He speaks approval, acceptance and love. Even in pain, confusion or hurt, let this truth become a well in your heart that never runs dry. Then, you will find yourself expressing sonship to the fullest as you say, "Not my will Father, but yours!"

STUDY GUIDE: CHAPTER 2
THE FIRST BORN

Relationship is different to religion.

*"The beginning of religion is here: let us work,
let us get to heaven, let us find identity."*

**Do you see any areas in your life where you live out of the law,
trying to earn your salvation and the Father's love rather than simply
receiving it?**

Throughout this chapter Carlos explains the journey of sonship. Jesus
is loved, He is promoted and He surrenders.

He is Loved

Read Mark 1:9–11.

**Can you hear the Father speaking this over you and receive it in
your heart?**

*You [insert your name] are my dearly loved son,
with you I am well pleased.*

Speak this phrase out loud and repeat it a number of times. You are loved just as you are, you don't have to do anything to receive this love. Does it sink in easy or meet with some resistance? If it feels harder to receive think about why. Give those things over to the Father.

He is Promoted

Read Mark 9:2-13. Jesus' response to the Father's love was obedience. When we walk in sonship we respond to the Father out of our love for him. Obedience is part of the overflow of our love for him, initiated by his love for us.

Is there any area of your life where the Father is calling you to obedience?

> "He is loved independently of his doing and He is promoted because He obeys. True sonship always finds a way to respond."

He Surrenders

Read Mark 14.

> "It is possible for us to trust the Father in our times of suffering, transition and decision. Jesus made a way for us now to be the ones who pray: "not my will, but yours!"

How easy do you find it to pray the prayer, "not my will, but yours?" A heart that is able to surrender is a heart that knows it is loved, accepted, and approved of. If surrender raised questions and doubts in you, return to the truth that He loves you and is well pleased with you.

CHAPTER THREE

DADDY ISSUES

Define yourself radically as one beloved by God. This is the true self.
Every other identity is illusion. — BRENNAN MANNING

What are we going to do with the following information? According to Doctor Daniel Amneus,[1] "Compared to children in male-headed traditional families, where their natural parents are married to each other, children living in any other environment, deprived of their natural fathers, are:

- 8 times more likely to go to prison
- 5 times more likely to commit suicide
- 10 times more likely to have behavioral problems
- 20 times more likely to become rapists
- 32 times more likely to run away

- 10 times more likely to abuse chemical substances
- 9 times more likely to drop out of high school
- 33 times more likely to be seriously abused
- 73 times more likely to be fatally abused
- One-tenth as likely to get A's in school
- On average, have a 44% higher mortality rate
- On average, have a 72% lower standard of living."

Add this data to the fact that more than 50% of marriages end up in divorce, and the math equals a serious problem. The reality that this statistic cannot confirm is that these issues are not just all around, as someone else's problem, they are on the inside of us. Yes, 100% of us have daddy issues. In an interview with leading psychiatrist, Dr. Richard Fitzgibbons, he explains that while the term "father wound" is not an officially recognized clinical term, it is used by mental health professionals in identifying the origin of numerous emotional and behavioral conflicts. These difficulties can be the result of failing to have a strong, loving and supportive relationship with a father. They can also be the result of repeating significant weaknesses of the father such as selfishness, excessive anger, emotionally distant behaviors, or indifference to the faith.

A child raised without a father will grow up with inner struggles and questions of identity, "What can I do? Who am I? Where do I fit?" And in this broken world of sin and pain, the answers given will mostly be incorrect. Our society is quietly proving that life for most adults is a frustrating search for the approval of their father from childhood; the man responsible for the protection, provision, nurture, and modeling during their formative years. Some of the most hurting people I have met are the product of a difficult or a nonexistent relationship with their earthly fathers. Most of my own brokenness is related to issues with my father. What about you?

The list goes from tough guys, who are trying to scare the world into seeing them as real men, to flirty girls who are trying to seduce the world with their beauty. Like professional athletes who receive approval from the crowd, or the artist who becomes addicted to the applause, we are all in a desperate pursuit of the acceptance of a father.

Corporate cowboys, angry coaches and religious manipulators are symptoms of what Doctor Frank Pittman calls in *Psychology Today*, *The Father Hunger.*[2] As society desperately searches to find nourishment for this ache, the simplest course has been to deny and discard the father figure altogether. Our culture has undervalued fatherhood, and now, we are paying the price.

It has become easier to reject the father figure than to deal with all the negative father types we have come across. They all seem to fit into one of these categories: the demanding father who expects perfection, the abusive father who wounds both the body and the heart, the absent father who is never there, the authoritarian father who controls us with rules, or the passive father who just doesn't care.

The relationship we've had with our father was the beginning of all relationships with men. He was the first man we knew, he set the tone for all the men who would come into our lives, and he delivered a deep message about who we were to him, and consequently who we were to the world. Our dads were a major force in determining our self-esteem. The father-child relationship starts with the child's earliest, most primitive feelings and expands from there to sophisticated thoughts, interactions and behaviors. And though these often continue on into adulthood and even parenthood, many of us as adults no longer recognize our feelings and actions as connected to our father's.[3]

We are now living out the legacy of wounds inflicted during our early years. Even those who had good fathers at home often go through a stage where they didn't want anything to do with them. This period of cold shoulders and distant relationship is often assumed to be a natural season of rebellion. We have accepted it as normal psychology or expected behavior. It is seen as the reality of every human being in one way or another because we can all relate to the emotions of pain, rejection, and disappointment that only a father figure can arouse.

The sad thing is that no matter how hard our parents tried to do their best, they were victims just like us, themselves hungry to be loved and accepted, but full of legitimate hurt and shame. And we bear witness to their wounds by being inflicted ourselves through them.

There are no caves to hide from these facts. Our need can only be met by the Papa who Jesus came to announce. "If you then, who are evil, know how to give good gifts to your children, how much more will your Father who is in heaven give good things to those who ask him!"[4] Jesus knows that earthly parents, although broken, are capable of a certain amount of good, but it is nothing compared to the goodness, the care and the provision of His ideal Father.

Therefore, this Father is willing and able to respond to our wound, our hunger, and even to the hurt that comes from a mother's rejection. As the Psalmist said, "For my *father* and my *mother* have forsaken me, but the LORD will take me in."[5]

Only God can take us into the home where abuse is *not* rampant, where expectations *are* healthy and where love *is* unconditional. He is a father to the fatherless and a mother to the rejected, "For as a mother comforts her child, so I will comfort you." [6] This is the promise of *El Shaddai* (the many-breasted-one) and for Him there is not a wound too deep to leave unhealed. It is for us to truly know the love of God the perfect parent, if not, we are going to expect someone else to make us feel special and worthy. We will look for something else to provide comfort. Someone else will define us, and they will be terribly wrong.

The Search for Significance

While modern studies help us give language to the father-wound and the father-hunger, the Scriptures are full of human stories about those who were in the quest for approval and identity. Many bible passages give us insight into the upbringing of its main characters; and that provides the perfect setup to demonstrate God's redemptive power, despite crazy families. In most of these hero's journeys, we meet them as broken sons or daughters who are rejected, confused and looking for meaning in their lives.

Specifically in Genesis we read the story of a man named: "The Leg Puller." You might know him as Jacob, the con-man who deceived his brother Esau out of the two most valuable things in ancient life: an inheritance, and the blessing of the father.

Jacob was born minutes after his twin brother but due to culture and personality, Esau is the one who becomes daddy's favorite. And this captivating story is about how Jacob did everything possible to earn what the favorite gets without trying.

While their father Isaac enjoyed Esau the hunter boy, Jacob

watched from inside a tent with a heart yearning for the same connection. There is no mention in the Bible of Isaac's love for his younger son, but it does state this cruel fact: "Isaac loved Esau, because he ate of his game."[7] Isaac is the father who loves one of his sons and the meals he makes.

Here are some basic human ethics: you are *not* meant to have favorites. Plus, it is super nice to eat with the whole family around the table. But Isaac, who himself was Abraham's favorite son, favored Esau and cherished eating alone with his best-loved boy. Not cool.

As Jacob watches this preferential treatment, he does not realize that he is a Bible figure who will become the subject of sermons for years to come. He has no clue that one day his name will be part of what identifies God on earth. He is just a boy, born thirty seconds too late, and his story reads like the movie plot of a bad family gathering that goes from bad to worse.

The Supplanter was fortunate to have a mother who heard God's leading about his destiny. While the young boy experienced unmerited rejection from dad, mom waited for the perfect moment to make *her* favorite son the one with the birthright and the blessing.

The right set of circumstances were presented and deception number one was achieved. The ideal combination of hunger and tiredness in Esau gave Jacob the opportunity to trade for his brother's birthright: all in exchange for a bowl of stew. This transaction tripled Jacob's inheritance, as he would take over the rights and double portion that were usually set aside for the eldest child. Jake hits the Jackpot! But the work was not finished when gaining the birthright. Jacob wanted more than just the possessions of the father—he was after his heart.

Years later, as Isaac grows old and blind, he made plans to give

Esau the coveted final blessing. This laying-on-of-hands would bestow upon him the promises of wealth, fertility, and prosperity. Isaac wanted some of Esau's hunting game first, and sent him off to bring back fresh meat to prepare dinner. While Esau was gone, Jacob's mom helped the youngest son craft a disguise. While she cooked the dinner Isaac was expecting from Esau, Jacob dressed up to look like his older brother. Deception number two was a bit more complicated, but for the first time in his life, Jacob would feel (and smell) like his hairy brother, and maybe experience what it is like being the favorite. Happiness awaits.

Just before going into the tent where Isaac waited, fear arose in Jacob because he understood how well his father knew his older brother. For years he saw them hunting and eating together. Countless times he heard them from a distance laughing and talking about God's promises. Jacob knew that if he were to be caught, his father would curse him on the spot! There would be no other reaction. He knew well how much Papa Isaac wanted this for awesome Esau.

But, in a mix of faith and fraud, the theater of pretend was complete. Jacob entered the tent, played his part just right and received his father's blessing.

How many of us continue to play dress-up in the hopes we will receive the father's blessing? We pretend to be someone we're not, and forget what God has said about us from the beginning. When will we stop denying the good in us and begin to accept our place as beloved creation? We were made for love, by all, in love.

You see, Jacob heard his dad speak words of honor about his life. Identity and future were released by this father of promise. Jacob was empowered as the first born son.

The problem is that Isaac's true desire was for Esau to remain as his beloved and blessed son. How could Jacob feel good about himself after what he did and how he did it? Yes, he had received the full blessing, but it still didn't change the fact that his father didn't want him, Isaac wanted his brother.

Moments later, when the deception is made known, Esau is furious and Isaac is powerless. To preserve Jacob's life, his parents send him off to a foreign land. He needs to get away from the older brother, who now walks as the rejected one in the land of their father, and is ready to kill his younger brother to recover the stolen identity.

Jacob goes far away and ends up in the land of Laban his uncle. There he falls in love with Rachel, his cousin, and in order to marry his love-at-first-sight, he was required to work for seven years as a shepherd in the fields. He works the whole term and earns the right to marry his dream girl, but now, he is the one who is deceived. After his wedding party, he wakes up in the morning to see that Rachel was switched with her older sister Leah. He has now consummated marriage to the wrong lady! So he stands as a man out-hustled by his new family. The principle of sowing and reaping is in full display when Jacob questions Laban about this deception and his father-in-law replies, that in his country, the *oldest* comes *first*.

Cheated out of love, and forced to work some more, Jacob finally gets to be with Rachel. Then, after years of hard labor and after parenting twelve sons birthed from four different women, Jacob decides to return home. Isaac his father, Rebekah his mother and Esau his brother are still alive in the land of Canaan. Jacob is now wealthy, fruitful and full of revelation. He has had different encounters with the God of his grandfather Abraham and he believes that something better is before him. He understands that his father-in-law will not give him what he's looking for, and with one final deception, he leaves his current situation to face the consequences of his past.

On his journey back, while Jacob fearfully prepares to reunite with his angry brother "he finds himself alone and a man wrestled with him till daybreak."[8]

In one of the most interesting stories in the Bible, Jacob goes toe to toe with what seems to be the Angel of the Lord. This supernatural being is physically fighting with him and is ready to finish the bout when Jacob grunts, "I will not let you go unless you bless me!"

Jacob ends up with a painful and surprising victory. His whole life has been a constant pursuit of this ultimate blessing but he does not know any way to receive it other than through struggle. His assumption is that he does not deserve it, but he wants it anyway (just as we do). Isaac's youngest son knows no other way to receive a gift, for he has always had to fight, outsmart and cheat. He is still yearning for the blessing, the affirmation and the acceptance. He knows deep inside that the blessing he got from his biological father was not truly intended so he is still fighting, still looking, still Jacob.

The only way he wins *this* fight is if "the man" himself allows him to win. He was raised as the weak one of the family but in this encounter Jacob struggles with God almighty, and he succeeds.

He was intentionally wounded by God so he would stop fighting, and this wounding becomes a sign of healing. It is the end of the struggle. He got a new way of walking, and with it, a new identity in the ultimate Father. Every step he took from that moment onwards was a limp into acceptance. The man with the swagger was now the man with the limp, and a man with a limp is a man you can trust.

Finally the man asked him, "What is your name?"

"Jacob," he answered. Then the man said, "your name will no longer be Jacob, but Israel, because you have struggled with God and with humans and have overcome." [9]

Heaven knows *your* story dear reader. You have struggled with God and with humans. Life has been unkind. People have been unfair. You have been trained to work hard for the father's blessing and you have been given names that relate to your broken past, not your glorious future. You have misunderstood God and His reasoning for your existence, while others have misunderstood and rejected your uniqueness. Yet, you have made it this far and God is ready to give you a new identity; you *will* overcome.

Jacob the supplanter became Israel the prince. This man who used deception to earn favor became the one who represented God's chosen and favored people. God showed Jacob that it is His will for him to be blessed, and that neither his brother Esau, nor his father Isaac can determine or sway his God given destiny. Abba has chosen him, not by his merit or because of anything he has done to deserve it, but simply because it is His will. It is the God of his fathers who has finally given him the love, the relationship, and the approval that he has been yearning for his entire life.

We all have a father wound. We are all hungry for a father's love. It's only in the place where we meet God face to face, that we can be healed and fed by our Father in Heaven. The process might feel like a lasting wound but the limp will become the sign of your encounter and the end of striving.

Smile now Israel. You have not been forgotten.

Fulfilling the Word

He will turn the hearts of the parents to their children,
and the hearts of the children to their parents;
or else I will come and strike the land with total destruction.

— MALACHI 4:6

This is the final passage in the Old Testament. Significantly, its promise—and its warning—give way for the New Testament, it's the gate to the coming Messiah. It implies that the brokenness in this world between children and fathers reflects the brokenness between humanity and God. Restoring relationship with the Father is in fact the very focus of God's saving power in this world. Thus Jesus came to reconcile humanity to His Father. According to Gordon Dalbey, "Nowhere in this world is the impetus for that reconciliation more keenly felt than in relationship with our earthly fathers. The father-wound portrayed in the Malachi text is the difference between what Dad has given you and what Father God wants to give you. Thus, every person bears its sting."[10]

This turning is necessary for spiritual awakening. The hearts of the fathers need to turn to the children and the hearts of the children need to turn to their fathers. The outcome otherwise is destruction, fatality and a world of pain.

The good news for us is that, ***He*** will turn the hearts of the parents and the children. It is the work of God in us. This is a prophetic word that reveals an Old Testament problem yet offers a New Testament solution. From Genesis to Malachi we see imperfect people who need the perfect Father.

We spoke of Jacob; the one rejected, unfavored, and sent away. After him came Joseph, the boy who *is* the favorite, but misuses his favor and creates jealousy amongst his brothers. His brothers are the broken men who are so hungry for the father's attention, that they get rid of the distraction. Moses is the abandoned baby, raised by the enemy as one of their own. Gideon is the son of Joash, hiding because of fear, and complaining in his father's house. Ruth is the Gentile immigrant who is desperate to belong. David is in the fields not being acknowledged as a son, and despised by his brothers before battle. Esther is the orphan girl who is adopted by her uncle and lives as a slave in the land of captivity.

We read of prophets and rulers and ordinary people who suffered the father wound, and carried the father hunger. They faced rejection in their homes and abuse by their loved ones, but it was in that place where God turned their hearts to Himself.

No matter what your growing-up scenario was, the need for God the Father is the same. And it is this Father who will turn our hearts towards Himself and, towards each other. It is His very Spirit who will make the promise of reconciliation a reality among us all. He is a master at turning hearts and all that is required is for us to allow Him.

The Guarantee

Thousands of years after Jacob, and 400 years after the promise of Malachi, one person was able to live with a non-reaction to the father-wound. Jesus Christ of Nazareth walked the earth as one who satisfied his father-hunger daily by living in Abba's will. His heart was turned towards His earthly parents and the fullness of His identity came from His Daddy in Heaven. It is Jesus who became the fulfillment of that last prophetic word and it is He who paid the price so our hearts could be turned again.

As a spiritual father Himself, Jesus called twelve men to be His followers. He chose them despite their insecurities, backgrounds and false identities. Peter, James, John, Judas and the others, all with their distinctive weaknesses and all in need of a healing touch.

After three years of fellowship and after days of private talks about His approaching death, Jesus promised them "I will not leave you as orphans; I will come to you." [11]

Jesus picked up the expectation of abandonment and unfulfilled promises that was percolating in their hearts. They were desperate to remain with the Christ, to gain favor in His kingdom and to become great among men. They were hungry for significance and saw this man as the King who would give them titles, power and value.

The problem was that the message Jesus was preaching was backwards. His methods were confusing. He kept inviting them to be servants of each other and encouraging them to be like little children. He cared for the poor while caring little for the opinion of the powerful. Also, Jesus was constantly exposing how dependent He was Himself. He was showing them a different way to succeed: surrender to the Father's love.

In this clash of mixed messages, these grown men had a legitimate fear of being left to fend for themselves. That assumption came from years of hearing the wrong sermons from the religious leaders of their time, for they preached a god who is angry and distant and hungry to judge. They had also just heard Jesus talk about one of them betraying the Son of Man, and about Peter himself denying his savior friend. Their confidence was shaky and their questions were not getting answered in a way they could comprehend. Abandonment was on the horizon and these boys needed to be assured.

They also had experiences in their own journeys with fathers who were not around and mothers who offered no comfort. They too carried the wound. So here they are in John 14, in need of assurance. And it comes through the sound of His voice. In the original Greek language, the passage reads like this: "I will not leave you fatherless; *I am coming to you.*"

His promise is true even today, **He is coming to you**. Right now, the one who has always been father and mother will approach your presence with His strength and comfort. The Great I am is overwriting the fear and the abandonment on your insides. You are not without a father, He is the eternal *coming to you.*

Jesus goes on to say, "And he who loves me will be loved by my Father, and I will love him and manifest myself to him." [12]

Confronted with your wound and hunger He will show Himself. This means that He will properly be present in the sight of your "daddy issues," your fear, your pain, your burdens, your questions and your doubts. And in that place, He will reveal who He is to you, and who you truly are to Him. You will be properly loved and He will demonstrate that love with His manifest presence. The inevitable result of hearing His words and encountering His goodness is that you will:

- have a 0% chance of being rejected by God
- be 100 times more likely to enjoy life

- be 10 times more likely to be at peace
- be 200 times more likely to forgive
- on average, have a 100% higher happiness rate
- 10 out of 10 times, we will be received
- have a 100% guaranteed inheritance of joy and grace.

As the angels declared on the night the Messiah was born, "Do not be afraid. **I bring you good news** that will cause great joy for all the people."[13] These are the statistics of the Kingdom and that is what you can expect from your Jesus above. Everyday and always.

STUDY GUIDE: CHAPTER 3
DADDY ISSUES

"Yes, 100% of us have daddy issues."

Can you relate to Carlos's statement about all of us having daddy issues?

Can you recognise behaviour in your own life where you are seeking the acceptance of a father? What does this look like for you?

Carlos lists different father types:

- The demanding father, who expects perfection
- The abusive father, who wounds both the body and the heart
- The absent father, who is never there
- The authoritarian father, who controls us with rules
- The passive father, who just doesn't seem to care

Which one of these types best describes your own father?

You may identify traits of more than one. Can you recognize and trace feelings and actions in your life back to the way you related to your father, and how they related to you?

"Fathers are responsible for our self-esteem."

Our parents are victims too. In acknowledging how they wounded us we are not dishonouring them.

"Our need can only be met by the Papa that
Jesus came to announce."
"It is for us to truly know the love of God the perfect parent, if not,
we are going to expect someone else to make us feel special and
worthy. We will look for something else to provide comfort. Some
one else will define us, and they will be terribly wrong."

Jacob and Esau

"How many of us continue to play dress up in the hopes we will
receive the Father's blessing?"

**Do you see in your own life the father wounds you carry and the
desire for a father's love?**

Regardless of our upbringing we need to know God the Father.
Read Jesus' words of comfort to the disciples in John 14 and let them
sink in.

"I will not leave you as orphans;
I will come to you." — JOHN 14:18
"His promise is true even today, he is coming to you"

CHAPTER FOUR

THE ORPHAN ANTIDOTE

God loves you exactly as you are!
But He loves you too much to leave you as you are.

— JOHN ARNOTT

Moses was an orphan in a basket, Superman is an orphan with a cape and Steve Jobs was the orphan who created. Aristotle grew up without his parents, Muhammad was abandoned at the age of six and Buddha became an orphan in his twenties. Cyrus the Great, Simón Bolivar, Babe Ruth, Malcolm X, Nelson Mandela, Marilyn Monroe, Joseph Smith, John Lennon—the list of renowned orphans is endless, and revealing.

Since ancient literature there has been a glorification of the orphan character. These types and personalities are extremely common as literary protagonists, as well as being highlighted in biographies throughout human history. Whether good or bad, our world system values the orphans for what they can accomplish on their own, without a mom or a dad. Now don't get me wrong, it's a beautiful thing when a person who has been denied the basic rights of being loved by their parents can rise up against their circumstances and do well. We honor the sacrifices of those who succeed even while being abandoned. But, whether fictional or factual, the common theme revealed by these stories is that we live in a fatherless world. And we are okay with it.

Hollywood, in turn, has become a prophet who exposes the contaminated human heart and the hardness of people's souls. The movie industry shares the deep dark secrets of the world and exposes them unsparingly to make a buck. While the cinematographers push the limits of what should be shown on screen, they collect the sorrows of a generation, turn them into art and scream to us, the church: "We need a Father to embrace us!"

You see it in different movies and television shows; from the 80's classic *Pretty in Pink*, to *Disney's Up, Batman Begins* and the comedy *Click*. The workaholic absent father is a recurring character in Spielberg's movies, including *Close Encounters of the Third Kind, Indiana Jones* and *Hook*. From Darth Vader's "I am your Father" revelation in *Star Wars* to *Finding Nemo's* restoration of the father-son-clownfish relationship, focus groups have proven that the "father wound" element is the most powerful catalyst for an emotional response in an audience. It can almost guarantee a tear.

Another example of how television has exploited the father-son relationship is *The Fresh Prince of Bel-Air* series with Will Smith. The whole premise of the show was that of an orphan son who was sent from the dangerous projects in Philadelphia to live in the secure home of his uncle and aunt in Bel-Air, Los Angeles. I had been a fan of this program through the 90's and still love to watch reruns, but there is one episode at the end of season 4 that got fixed into my mind. It was titled, *"Papa's Got a Brand New Excuse"* and it is one of the few that used more of an emotional build-up than a comedy set up.

In it, Will is reunited with his father, Lou, for the first time in fourteen years. Uncle Phil has a hard time trusting Lou after he abandoned Will and his mother when he was a child. Will finally spends some quality time with his father and Lou shares the excuses of why he abandoned his family. Will forgives him and gives him a second chance. Uncle Phil can see that the real reason why Lou wanted to see Will was not for his son's best interest, but for his own but Will has a hard time believing that and he and Uncle Phil have a heated falling out and, as Will says, "Who cares what you think? You are not my father!" However, in the last scene when Will is packed and ready to leave with his father on a road trip, Lou explains that there is a job that is very important and he cannot fit his son in the journey. "I'm sorry son, I'll see you around," said the constantly absent father. Will nods his heads in shame and replies with cold disappointment, "Goodbye ... Lou." He realizes that this man is not his real father, and has to let him walk out of his life, again.

As Lou walks out Uncle Phil says to his nephew, "Will, it's all right to be angry." Will replies, "Hey, why should I be mad? I'm sayin' at least he said, 'Goodbye' this time. You know what? You ain't got to do nothing, Uncle Phil. It ain't like I'm still five years old, you know? Ain't like I'm gonna be sittin' up every night asking my mom 'When's Daddy coming home?', you know? *Who needs him?* Hey, he wasn't there to teach me how to shoot my first basket, but I learned, didn't I? And I got pretty damn good at it, too! Got through my first date without him, right? I learned how to drive, I learned how to shave, I learned how to fight without him! I had *fourteen* great birthdays without him! He never sent me a damn card! To hell with him!!! I didn't need him then and I don't need him now."

As agitated as his nephew is, Uncle Phil tries to reach out, "Will, Will?" But Will responds, "No, you know what, Uncle Phil? I'm gonna get through college without him, I'm gonna get a great job without him, I'm-a marry a beautiful honey and I'm havin' me a whole bunch of kids. I'll be a better father than he ever was! And I sure as Hell don't need him for that, cause there ain't a damn thing he could ever teach me about how to love my kids!"

After a long pause; and the present reality settling in, Will begins to cry and says, "How come he don't want me, man?" and for the first time ever, Uncle Phil and Will embrace as father and son.

In that last scene, it becomes obvious in Will Smith's eyes and voice that there was not much acting required. Smith himself comes from a broken home yet he has accomplished remarkable success as an actor, musician and humanitarian. His children are involved in acting work with him and their family appears to be one of the most solid ones in Hollywood. No matter the many things that can be achieved without it though, the heart will always yearn for our father's approval. It is in our nature to always want them, to want us.

The Orphan Spirit

When that desire to be wanted is not met with unconditional love, most humans will make the unconscious choice to live as an orphan.

Jack Frost, a champion of the Father Heart theology explains it like this, "The orphan spirit causes one to live life as if he does not have a safe and secure place in the Father's heart. He feels he has no place of affirmation, protection, comfort, belonging, or affection. Self-oriented, lonely, and inwardly isolated, he has no one from whom to draw Godly inheritance. Therefore, he has to strive, achieve, compete, and earn everything he gets in life. This easily leads to a life of anxiety, fears, and frustration."

So we use the term 'orphan spirit' to refer to a person who thinks, talks, acts and feels as if he has no Father to love him, no Savior to make him righteous, and no Holy Spirit to walk with him.

In my own life, this acknowledgement of the orphan spirit was a constant source of frustration. I found myself going from teaching to teaching and from ministry time to ministry time finding out how much of an orphan I was. I could not contain the striving and the competition. I was consumed with getting my own way and trying to succeed by my own efforts. I was never happy with myself, so I needed to find happiness in my work.

But I wanted a way to catch my behavior, to expose the lies and recognize the fatherless mindset. So I came up with my top-ten personal markers to single out the orphan spirit; a self-revelatory list to help me identify the lies I believed. Rewriting them was a painful exercise (as I still see some patterns) so I hope they are useful to you today:

1. When your envy grows because of others' success.
2. When you constantly criticize your leaders and those who are ministering or serving.

3. When you compare your accomplishments or your failures with those of others.

4. When you can't find time to serve unless there is recognition.

5. When you hide your sin and mistakes, and continue to pretend.

6. When you feel uncomfortable and out of place while surrounded by family and friends.

7. When you push for something that does not bring peace to those around you.

8. When you seek comfort in counterfeit affections such as addictions and compulsions.

9. When you move forward independently of God's leading or others' counsel.

10. When you manipulate people to change their decisions and attitudes with the use of your methods and spirituality.

In his book *Sons and Daughters*,[1] pastor Brady Boyd explains that, "Orphans focus solely on who they know, where they have been, what they have accomplished, what they are working on now, all the many rules they are dutifully following, and how long it has been since their last sin."

When the orphan mindset reaches the heart it will be easy to build walls, shift blame and justify gossip. The orphan will focus on visible duties only, while attitudes and deeper motivations will not get examined. He will constantly measure himself according to the opinion of other people and He will feel the weight of rejection even when others are extending acceptance.

What the Orphan Needs

In 2003, I met a man ruined by love. He was an all-American Jersey boy who was struggling with his health but decided on the spot to leave his world behind and respond to God's invitation to Russia.

What compelled Ethan to drop everything and move to the other side of the world was hearing the results of a study comparing the emotional and physical well being of institutionalized children with those adopted or placed in foster homes. The study suggested, "Children who passed the first two years in an orphanage had a lower IQ and attenuated brain activity compared with foster children or those never institutionalized." [2]

Furthermore, American scientists who compared recent studies in Eastern Europe with older US history discovered a worse toll on institutionalized children. A hundred years ago, one-third of babies in orphanages in the United States died before they reached seven months of age. To fight these odds, unwanted babies were brought to institutions where antiseptic procedures and adequate food promised a fighting chance for a healthy life. However, the orphans died, not from infectious diseases or malnutrition, but simply wasted away in a condition called marasmus. Sterile surroundings did not prevent it. Having enough food made no difference. These babies died by the thousands from the deprivation of human touch. Skin to skin contact was all that was required.

When an infant falls below the threshold of the physical affection needed to stimulate the production of growth hormones and the development of the immune system, his body starts to shut down.

When babies were removed from the clean, but impersonal institutions to environments where they could receive physical nurturing, the *marasmus* reversed. Babies that were being touched gained weight. Little ones being held finally began to increase in size and strength. Getting touched was all the orphans needed.

By the time we first met Ethan, it had been a year since he moved to Russia. He could not possibly bring the thousands of orphans living in orphanages back to America but he was convinced that one compassionate embrace every day could help them not just survive, but thrive. Since the primary need of an orphan is to be touched, for months, he would daily get up from his cold one bedroom apartment in St. Petersburg, to visit orphanages. Ethan would sit on a chair, and for long hours wait for children to form a line. One by one, the kids drew near to receive a hug. He could barely speak their language, but this young man found a way to be a healing father to God's little children.

Similarly, Matthew 19:14 narrates an occasion when parents had the genius idea to bring their kids close to Jesus for Him to lay his hands on them. He rebuked his own disciples when they tried to keep the little ones away, "Let the children come to me and do not hinder them." And according to scripture, He stayed till all the children had been touched and blessed.

Then, Jesus used the occasion to encourage His followers to act like these cuties, "For to such belongs the kingdom of heaven." Just as John reclined at the table and came close to His chest, only the ones who are similar in attitude, in confidence and in desire for proximity will feel the heartbeats of Love Himself.

These patterns that hinder us from being healthy in our hearts are not cured by more trying or more doing. They require an encounter with a good, touchy-feely Father (Remember Luke 15?)

You can change the orphan mindset with its attitudes and expectations. Just get in line and let God the Father reverse your *marasmus*. He is willing to hold you in the arms of unfailing love.

> *I will be a father to you, and you shall be sons and daughters to me,*
> *says the Lord Almighty.* — 2 CORINTHIANS 6:18 (ESV)

What the Orphan Wants

I met the Father during my second week at Catch The Fire Toronto, formerly Toronto Airport Christian Fellowship. I joined their School of Ministry in 2001 having left the pre-med program at the University of Puerto Rico. My plan was to get filled with the revival fire that would get me more anointed and famous (for the glory of Jesus of course), but soon after my arrival, I realized that the leaders were more concerned with the heart than with success in ministry.

I went in search of power and glory, but the curriculum was designed for healing and surrender. Bummer.

Their plan was to set us up for encounters with God, and on this day of my second week in Toronto, the teaching intended just that. After sharing for two hours on God's love, Peter and Heather Jackson invited us students to close our eyes and picture heaven. The Holy Spirit was supposed to take over and show us an image that would speak to our hearts, but I struggled to see anything. And like a Puerto Rican in a Canadian winter, I quickly felt out of place and numb.

The instrumental music in the background was inviting, Peter's voice was soft while instructing, and everyone seemed to be on board with this spiritual exercise—except me. Unexpectedly, as I questioned the format and the ministry, I saw myself in front of the white throne.

As I observed the surroundings with the eyes of my heart, I put my face down and noticed my own skin. I stood naked in heaven! So shame began to engulf me. In a split second, every sin committed in previous years was played back to me like a movie in fast forward. I became aware of how dirty I had arrived to this holy place and begged God to send me back. As I lifted my head, ready to be zapped, I noticed a finger stretched forward, like that of a caring mother beckoning her kids to draw near for fresh made cookies.

I had no clue what to do. I could barely agree that these images in my head were an admissible experience. My imagination was used to lustful thoughts, plots of vengeance and plans for the execution of a lie; but not to seeing heaven. This was unnatural and uncomfortable, so why keep going with it?

Nonetheless, I had a thought that bypassed my brain and went straight into my heart. As clear as the sound of my own voice, I heard the words "you are forgiven." The voice sounded just like the Jesus that found me at the Billy Graham crusade in 1995. The feeling was just like the Holy Spirit that filled me up with heavenly language at youth camp in 1996.

Then I understood that the sin in front of me was not displayed as a humiliation exercise, but to reveal the greatness of His love; the same love that asked me to come closer whilst I stood naked in heaven.

It was six years after my born-again experience, and I had no clue that the finger, the grace and the throne belonged to God the Father.

As I began to move closer towards Him, I noticed something on my back. A purple and white mantle rested on my shoulders. It looked like a royal robe. I was now fully dressed and standing tall. The feelings of embarrassment stopped as I began to walk at a faster pace to Him. I started to get excited about the possibility of this being a legitimate thing. But, as I tried to increase my speed, I tripped on the massive robe I wore. It was too big for me; God had clothed me with His own gown.

"Who knew you could fall in heaven?" I thought, and before I even had the chance to analyze the event through the lens of my "there-is-no-falling-in-heaven" theology, I heard a rumbling. The Ancient of Days got up from His throne, put his arm around my waist, picked me up from the floor, and sat me on His lap. I felt inexplicably welcomed, and I knew that I had arrived home.

In a moment, the rush of emotions that crowded my soul manifested physically through groans and shivers and I began to cry out loud with my eyes hard shut.

So many things to say; I could not stop talking! In this face to face meeting with God I was driven to ask for the anointing to heal the sick. I asked Him to save my family and friends. I told Him how much I wanted to be in the ministry, do crusades, plant churches, bring revival, save the world. And through the lightning fast prayers, the Father kept attentive and nodding. He displayed a genuine smile, like the expression of a grandpa who listens to the ramblings of an excited 2-year-old. Then suddenly I realized God Almighty, the ultimate voice in the universe, was in front of me. So I stop my desperate pleas with a deep breath and gave Him my "I'm ready to listen" face.

The Father looked into my eyes and said, "Carlos, I don't need you to be a pastor, I don't need you to save the lost or heal the sick. I don't need you to do crusades or bring revival. All I want is for you to be my son."

My Son.

I found God, the Father of Jesus, and He was revealed to me as God, the Father of Carlos. His words healed old pain stored in my depths, and for the first time in my life, I was convinced … *He loves me!* Not because of what I do, but because of who I am.

And, it's because of who I am that I get to enjoy my full inheritance as a son.

Sobs and snot became leaked abundantly as my weeping lost all boundaries. For the next two hours, as I shared my thoughts with God fearlessly, I was surprised at how fun-loving *Abba* is. We talked baseball stats, His favorite foods (Thai being number one) and how much He liked my drumming. As Jesus stroked my head and spoke to the Father about my life, I sat on God's right knee and absorbed the glory of this moment.

Remaining doubts about this experience being legitimate were dissipated, when Stephan, my small group leader, sat next to me. I had known this German pastor for less than two weeks and I did not expect him to pick me up and sit me on his lap. But that is what He did. Exactly as the Father had done. And that occurrence (which was the perfect scenario for me to be weirded-out of Toronto) became the best confirmation of God's love. My soaking face got imprinted on his T-shirt as he held me and prayed quietly for what seemed like eternity. After he moved on to pray for others, I kept on crying, laughing, shaking and enjoying this radical moment with Daddy God. Everything I thought I knew about love was revolutionized that day.

The presence of God surrounded me for weeks afterwards. Every day, I would run back to that place in my mind and approach Him as a little kid who is eager to hang out with his dad. The more time I spent with Him, the more I realized how much He cared. He cared about the pain I carried towards my own father and He led me to forgive from the heart. He knew of the issues with my mom and sisters, and He showed me how He loved them. He cared about my passion for my calling so He taught me how to surrender.

Now I ask: If good things are in store for those who believe, why are we so afraid to trust as little children? Why would we not believe that God is willing and able to manifest Himself in a personal way? The Bible says that, "What no eye has seen, nor ear heard, nor the heart of man imagined, what God has *prepared* for those who love him—these things God has *revealed* to us through the Spirit." [3] What is unfamiliar does not necessarily mean it's unbiblical. The way to properly know a tree is by its fruit (not by its look).

Abba Father wants to manifest Himself to you. He wants to speak to you. He is the same God who revealed himself to Adam and Eve in the cool of the day; to Moses in the burning bush; to David through songs and poems; to Elijah in the sound of a whisper; to Paul in an open vision. Yet, as Pastor John Arnott likes to say, "Sometimes we believe more in the devil's ability to deceive us, than in God's ability to reveal Himself to us."

This life altering relationship, abundant in experiences, is available to us because of what Jesus has already done. These encounters are part of what He still does for us. And the Son Jesus is now the open road to these moments. "No one comes to the Father except through me."[4]

What the Orphan Gets

In the natural realm we wait until our parents die before we collect our inheritance. By that time, most brothers and sisters become enemies as they deal with the process of deciding what is their fair share. In the kingdom of Heaven, our Father will never die and there is no need to fight for our portion of the pie. Our spiritual inheritance is available from the moment we said *yes* to Jesus. On top of that, we get the full rights, blessings and properties of the Father as if we were the only son. Being the first born son is not a male or female thing, it is a gift received in faith by those who believe.

As Paul wrote, "For you did not receive the spirit of slavery to fall back into fear, but you have received the Spirit of adoption as sons, by whom we cry, 'Abba! Father!' The Spirit himself bears witness with our spirit that we are children of God, and if children, then heirs—heirs of God and fellow heirs with Christ, provided we suffer with him in order that we may also be glorified with him."[5]

The Central Event was about your justification; it is the testimony of your right standing with God. Adoption is about inclusion, it is the testimony of being a member of His family. Intentionally, Paul uses ancient Roman adoption as the analogy to explain our belonging in the Father:

In the first century, the *patria potestas* was the father's legal power to control or even dispose of his children. A Roman son never came of age in regard to his father. No matter how old, the offspring remained under the absolute possession and control of the father. This Roman concept of fatherhood made adoption a very difficult and serious step. A person had to be transferred from one *patria potestas* to another; out of the possession and control of one father into the equally absolute possession and control of another.

Roman adoption was a two-step process and it was mostly used to redeem slaves. The first step was known as *mancipatio*, and it was carried out by a symbolic sale in which the *patria potestas* was held to be broken. A ceremony called *vindicatio* followed after completion of the sale. The adopting father would go to one of the Roman magistrates and present a legal case for the transference of the slave into his possession. When the process was completed, in the presence of seven witnesses, the *vindicatio* (adoption) was absolute. From that moment onwards the person was undeniably a son. If that sonship was ever in doubt, the son would have seven witnesses who would validate the adoption and confirm his placement in the father's house.

Nonetheless, it is the consequences of Roman adoption, which are most significant within the process. Check this out from Barclay's daily Bible study: The adopted person lost all rights to his old family and gained all the rights as a fully legitimate son to his new family. He got a new father in the most literal sense and in the most legally binding way. The adopted son became heir to his new father's estate and He was inalienably a co-heir. Even if other sons, real blood relations, were born afterwards it did not affect his rights. In law, the old life of the adopted person was completely wiped out and all legal debts were cancelled as though they had never been. The adopted person was regarded as a new person entering into a new life, and in the eyes of the law the adopted person was literally and absolutely the son of the new father.

The most beautiful thing about this adoption illustration is that once the individual was adopted, that new son could never be returned to slavery. There was no expiration date to his acceptance. There was no legal precedent in Roman law for undoing the adoption. A Roman father could deny his own children and sell them to slavery through *mancipatio*, but he could never return those he gain through *vindicatio*.

And so it is with God.

You are not a slave to the fear of being rejected, abandoned or denied. You can sincerely call out His name *Abba* and know that you have been adopted into His family. Then, it is the Holy Spirit who acts as a witness to the adoption ceremony. He is the one who will continue to share that testimony with your spirit. It is not for you to convince yourself of sonship, but the Spirit of Truth who reminds you of who you are right now in Christ Jesus.

No matter who comes to deny your placement in the household, God's Spirit acting as the seven witnesses will testify of what has already happened. He has legal proof that you are loved and that you belong. He has seen the Father love you through the son Jesus and He is now the Spirit of this Adoption.

> *And hope does not put us to shame, because God's love has been poured out into our hearts through the Holy Spirit, who has been given to us.* — ROMANS 5:5

Are you willing to be embraced out of the orphan mindset and into a happy (and eternal) sonship? I guarantee you, there is no theology clever enough and no testimony powerful enough to substitute your own personal encounter with the Father. It is time for the Holy Spirit to share with you a story. As the eyes of your heart are enlightened, He will recount the personal testimony of your Adoption moment.

Seriously, stop reading.

Turn your eyes to heaven, look up to the throne of grace and listen to the sound of His voice … Go close.

The Orphan Spirit

When we don't know and experience the unconditional love of the Father we live like orphans. It is in our nature for us all to want our fathers' approval, and for them to want us.

Jack Frost describes the orphan spirit:

> The orphan spirit causes us to live life as if he does not have a safe and secure place in the Father's heart. He feels he has no place of affirmation, protection, comfort, belonging or affection. Self-oriented lonely, and inwardly isolated, he has no one from whom to draw Godly inheritance. Therefore, he has to strive, achieve, compete and earn everything he gets in life. This easily leads to a life of anxiety, fears and frustration.

Can you see yourself in the words of this definition?
We can become so accustomed to the lies and mindsets that living as an orphan creates, that we don't even notice they are there.

Read Carlos' list of orphan spirit markers in the chart ahead. Each of these markers reflects an orphan spirit characteristic. **Do you relate**

to any of these in your own life? When you look at the chart ask Holy Spirit to show you the ways in which you live like an orphan.

Carlos tells his story of the first time he encountered the Father's loving embrace, and knew for the first time he was a son.

1. What is your response to his encounter?
2. Do you believe God can manifest himself to you in a similarly personal way?
3. If you do, great! Make space and ask him to come to you.
4. If you don't, are you able to identify why you don't? And how this could be holding you back? Talk to the Father about these things.

Justification is about your right standing with God. Many Christian's get this part and accept Jesus as their saviour but they never fully live in his family, experiencing adoption. The Father has adopted you into his family. You are a co-heir with Christ. Everything the Father has is your inheritance.

Ask the Holy Spirit to come and recount to you your personal testimony of adoption.

THE HEART OF AN ORPHAN		THE HEART OF SONSHIP
See God as Master	IMAGE OF GOD	See God as a loving Father
Independent/Self-reliant	DEPENDENCY	Interdependent/Acknowledges Need
Live by the Love of Law	THEOLOGY	Live by the Law of Love
Insecure/Lack peace	SECURITY	Rest and Peace
Strive for the praise, approval, and acceptance of man	NEED FOR APPROVAL	Accepted in God's love, justified by grace
A need for personal achievement as you seek to impress God and others, or no motivation to serve at all	MOTIVE FOR SERVICE	Service that is motivated by a deep gratitude for being unconditionally loved and accepted by God
Duty and earning God's favor or no motivation at all	MOTIVE BEHIND CHRISTIAN DISCIPLINES	Pleasure and delight
"Must" be holy to have God's favor, thus increasing a sense of shame and guilt	MOTIVE FOR PURITY	"Want to" be holy; do not want anything to hinder intimate relationship with God
Self-rejection from comparing yourself to others	SELF-IMAGE	Positive and affirmed because you know you have such value to God
Seek comfort in counterfeit affections: addictions, compulsions, escapism, busyness, hyper-religious activity	SOURCE OF COMFORT	Seek times of quietness and solitude to rest in the Father's presence and love
Competition, rivalry, and jealousy toward others' success and position	PEER RELATIONSHIPS	Humility and unity as you value others and are able to rejoice in their blessings and success

Accusation and exposure in order to make yourself look good by making others look bad	**HANDLING OTHERS' FAULTS**	Love covers as you seek to restore others in a spirit of love and gentleness
See authority as a source of pain; distrustful toward them and lack a heart attitude of submission	**VIEW OF AUTHORITY**	Respectful, honoring; you see them as ministers of God for good in your life
Difficulty receiving admonition; you must be right so you easily get your feelings hurt and close your spirit to discipline	**VIEW OF ADMONITION**	See the receiving of admonition as a blessing and need in your life so that your faults and weaknesses are exposed and put to death
Guarded and conditional; based upon others' performance as you seek to get your own needs met	**EXPRESSION OF LOVE**	Open, patient, and affectionate as you lay your life and agencas down in order to meet the needs of others
Conditional & Distant	**SENSE OF GOD'S PRESENCE**	Available & Intimate
Bondage	**CONDITION**	Liberty
Feel like a Servant/Slave	**POSITION**	Feel like a Son/Daughter
Spiritual ambition; the earnest desire for some spiritual achievement and distinction and the willingness to strive for it; a desire to be seen and counted among the mature.	**VISION**	To daily experience the Father's unconditional love and acceptance and then be sent as a representative of His love to family and others.
Fight for what you can get!	**FUTURE**	Sonship releases your inheritance!

CHAPTER FIVE

THE OTHER "FATHER"

Our problem with faith is not the inability to hear His voice,
it is the willingness to hear others.

— BILL JOHNSON

Satan is the first orphan. He was kicked out of heaven, never to return. He rose against the True Father in an attempt to become superior, fought for a glory that did not belong to him and lost his place of influence as a servant of light. Lucifer proclaimed, "I will place my throne above the stars and I will be like the Most High (God)."[1] Imagine the pride it takes to leave all that goodness! And with it, he was driven mad by rebellion and rallied a third of the angels to futility.

Today he rules in a lowly chair in the place God created for such iniquity. He became the tempter, the lord of the flies and the enemy of God. Eternally defeated and hungry for revenge, he now lurks as a toothless lion. Jesus took away his bite but he will use "the lie" as his weapon of choice and treat each of us, as his next potential victim. "Because you are unable to hear what I say. You belong to your father, the devil, and you want to carry out your father's desires. He was a murderer from the beginning, not holding to the truth, for there is no truth in him. When he lies, he speaks his native language, **for he is a liar and the father of lies.**" [2]

Jesus explained to the religious leaders, that their inability to hear His words implied submission to another voice. Subsequently, if the role of a father is to give identity to the children, then Satan's main role is to give his false identity to his illegitimate sons and daughters. The first orphan became a father and his seed of deceit has been planted in all who hear his voice. He is supremely the Orphan Maker; the one who denies you and makes you eternally unhappy.

The deception of glory that Lucifer believed became in the garden of Eden, the temptation he used against Adam and Eve. "Eat of the fruit and you will be like God (the Most High)," the serpent asserted. The first humans lived in the paradise of relationship with a mission to rule. They had no need for the serpent's proposal for they were already like God. Still they accepted the venom of doubt, ate the fruit of the wrong tree, and brought death to humankind.

The enemy's strategy was simple, question the goodness of the Creator and distort the value of those created. Satan made them think that they were missing out from being superior, as if God had failed to create them perfectly. He lied to Adam and Eve and said, "Eat, you will certainly not die" contradicting the warning of their Caretaker. He got them to believe that God was holding back a greater life in the forbidden tree. His deception reduced the Father in the eyes of His beloved creation to a cheap master who keeps good things from his slaves.

By listening to the enemy, their perception was changed. His lies made them see differently, for the tree never looked good before then. Unfortunately for us, the first humans listened to the cunning arguments and acted in agreement with the lies. Both man and woman were seduced by power and deceived into entering the state of orphanhood.

However, God approached Adam and Eve in the cool of the day. Even after that bite, He planned to have an evening stroll with His boy and His girl. God already knew the answer, but He calls out lovingly to them: "Where are you?"

Adam replies, "We heard you and we were afraid because we were naked, so we hid."

The lie that initiated them in disobedience now gives them the unknown taste of fear and shame. Here is the first ever experience of fear and it is the experience of two people being scared of the lovely voice of God. What a tragedy to humanity that the first negative self-conscious thought of the created son and daughter, was seeing their own naked bodies and being ashamed.

"Who told you, you were naked?" God asked carefully, knowing the answer. "The woman you put here with me—she gave me some fruit from the tree, and I ate it," Adam replied, with the first ever, *blame-the-wife, blame-God* reaction.

The Lord God asks the woman, "What is this you have done?" "The serpent deceived me, and I ate," she replied with the classic *blame-the-devil* response.

But, Eve was right. They ate from the tree because they first listened to the liar. By believing the deception and acting upon it, all of us have been affected by sin, sickness and death.

That is how Satan became a father. The original orphan deceived the children of God into becoming orphans themselves, slaves to the one whom they obeyed.[3] Now, we are the ones who fear God's voice, we are the ones that hide in the garments of shame, we are the ones who are unhappy with ourselves and we are the ones who struggle to find a home.

It was here in the first Adam where we were all escorted out of the garden and launched into this long journey of rediscovering who we are, and it is here outside of paradise where we decide who our father truly is.

Listen to Your True Father

The most powerful thing a parent can speak over their children is true identity. God, as a master in fatherhood, teaches us to believe the best and encourages us to speak it out, "Let the weak say he is strong!" even when circumstances defy the truth.

As we saw in chapter two, Jesus came out of the waters after being baptized in the River Jordan, and the Father spoke identity over Him (*This is my beloved son in whom I am well pleased* ...) yet immediately after, the Spirit led Jesus to the desert and for forty days, God the Son fasted, prayed, walked, trusted and waited.

Obviously Jesus got hungry, and while in the wilderness Satan was given the opportunity to tempt Him in what appeared to be the weakest moment of His human life. After multiple failed attempts to kill Jesus during his early years, Satan wanted to use the most powerful strategy compiled in hell to eliminate Him once and for all. He could have used lust to tempt the 30-year-old virgin. He could have used bitterness since the Son was taken to the desert to go hungry and be alone. There were many options for the devil to choose from; different temptations and nasty schemes. But Satan had one plan. His greatest tactic, and the one used against his greatest enemy, was to challenge the words the Father had already spoken.

"If you really are the Son of God," was the opening remark, strategically chosen by the father of lies, for the temptation against Jesus. And against you.

First, Satan asks Him to turn a rock into bread, because "a good Father would never allow His son to go hungry ... Right?"

During the second temptation, he offered Jesus a chance to prove how much his Father loved Him. Satan asked Jesus to throw himself down from the temple in Jerusalem. "Jump!" He said. "The scripture says He will catch you, you know? Since your Father is so good and all."

And finally, he presented Jesus the kingdoms of the world. "If you really are the Son of God ... Then your Father would have given you all the things I am now offering. Because surely He who claims to be your a daddy would never deny you from having power and influence over the world that belongs to Him ... Or, am I wrong?"

Jesus was able to defeat the temptation because He knew who He truly was, who His Father was, and how much that Father loved Him. That was the food he was eating for forty days, the very words that came from the mouth of His Father.

You see, if the enemy is able to challenge our sonship in a way that can make us question the goodness of our Father, his work to make us fall into any other kind of sin is achieved. The father of lies has no intention of pushing our hand to do the wrong thing. His strategy is to convince us of our wrong value, for sinning is natural if we believe we are sinners (as sonship will be natural when we believe we are God's sons).

The bible summons us to come under heaven's arrangement and combat the accusations until we see victory. "Submit yourselves, then, to God. Resist the devil, and he will flee from you." [4] In this verse, James uses the word *diablos* which means: *the false accuser, unjustly criticizing to cause hurt, condemn and sever a relationship.*

Yep. Sounds like him.

It's the same enemy who came to the garden of Eden, and to the desert of temptation, to sever the father-son relationship. Adam and Eve failed to resist. But Jesus was able to submit *and* resist; and according to the Bible, this is also possible for you and me.

The first thing we do when we start a conversation with someone meaningful is that we stop other conversations. So if the plan is to make the devil flee, then we shall close our ears to his hellish accusations and surrender to the words spoken by God. Because it's the truth uttered by a perfect Father that will change the outcome of our battles. God is willing and able to change the doubts, the bitterness, and the fear. However, while God speaks truth to our hearts day by day, the enemy speaks lies to our minds constantly. And the way we manage our daily thoughts, determines which father we get our identity from.

Two fathers have walked into the orphanage of our heart. One is lovely and caring and the other is mean and unforgiving. The one who growls rejects us and whispers nasty things about our image, our value and our personality. The one with the smile receives us with a kiss and welcomes us with a hug. According to the first letter of John, God is love. And, according to 1 Corinthians 13 *love believes, hopes, and endures all things.* That means that when we become the recipients of this love—the greatest love of all—Love himself believes, endures, and hopes in us, and for us.

Every time we draw near to repent, God believes us to be genuine. He receives every prayer of surrender as a fragrant offering. Whenever we have fallen into sin, He has endured with us. The all-knowing Father does not respond to our words as a cynical man would. He does not look into our future and complain about upcoming failures. When we talk, He believes. When we pray, He hopes. When we fall, He endures. His love never fails.

Satan has come to kill, steal and destroy. He wants you to continue eating from the tree of the knowledge of good and evil but the Father has set a table before you in the presence of your enemies. Whose meals are you going to eat? Whose voice are you going to listen to? Which one will father you today?

It Starts with Belief

Most of the ungodly emotions we experience originated in a dirty lie we believed. Therefore, to see change in these reactions we first must tackle the root; and this all starts with one essential truth.

The most important thing you could ever do, is *to believe in Jesus.* Just as all of our ungodly emotions originate in a lie, eternity is determined by your childlike acceptance of the gift of salvation. When you declare who Jesus is and believe in your heart that He is alive for you, the destination of your soul changes forever. Eternity is ruled by one single belief. According to Romans 10:9-11, "If we declare with our mouth, 'Jesus is Lord,' and believe in our hearts that God raised him from the dead, we will be saved. For it is with our heart that we believe and are justified, and it is with our mouth that we profess our faith and are saved."

You are chosen. You have been forgiven. You are a new creation. Do you believe it? Knowing this information is valuable; believing it is indispensable.

Imagine this scenario: The most horrible human, Satan's greatest masterpiece, is a rapist of women and children who has never exhibited an ounce of regret, and today he's in a local hospital about to die.

Vengeful and angry, he thinks back and enjoys the memories of a lifetime hurting others. Since his first day of consciousness, he has manifested hatred towards everyone and rebellion has been his modus operandi. Theft, gossip, murder and violence are all part of his celebrated identity. Even as death arrives to win the battle, he is looking for one last victim to harass. And finally, during his last hour, an older nurse approaches him carefully with a glass of water.

Yet somehow, the man cannot be cruel. The way she smells and walks invite him to stop the hunt and reply instead with a half grumbled, "Thank you." The words taste unusual, but her kindness warms his heart.

The nurse knows all about his cold, lonely journey. After hearing news of his capture, the hospital staff have been talking about him all week long. The doctors are happy to let him suffer and the other nurses refuse to treat him. They give him a lesser dosage of morphine than they would have given to other patients in the same condition. Not one soul has come to visit. His sad end feels like justice but this soft-spoken nurse, willing to override the past, smiles back and says, "You're welcome."

He cannot remember the last time anyone spoke calmly to him and he is glad that she starts a conversation. On and on she goes, chatting about her grandkids and Jesus, heaven and hell, food and music. He is confused as to why he wants to listen, but he does.

When she finally offers to pray together, he cannot help but nod a yes. She feels giddy for the victory and can sense God's presence invading the room. As a soft whisper he repeats the words she slowly says and on his very last breath on earth, the most horrible human being feels forgiven.

Do you believe this man will enjoy eternal life in heaven? Just like you and me? Forever and ever? Do you agree that He will be in paradise with Jesus if he declared with his mouth and believed in his heart?

Salvation is not about what we do, it's about whom we believe in. Getting to heaven is not about saying the right things, but about confessing the Right One. We get to experience eternity in the Father's delight not by any single act of self-righteousness but by the One who remained righteous till the end. Jesus fulfilled the law perfectly so that we could get filled with Him completely. Any other story is a fabricated lie. Huge BS from hell. We know this to be scripturally accurate because the first recorded person to become a resident of heaven was the thief who hanged next to Jesus. They died minutes apart. One with a perfect record, the other with a long list of faults. In the gospels of Matthew and Mark we hear of both criminals mocking the Christ between them but the gospel of Luke shares a change of heart in one of them; a moment where the thief who deserves the cross discovers grace. Both criminals have received judgment according to the law, both are experiencing the penalty for their sins, only one makes the choice to believe. And because of that one belief, both he and Jesus have been together in paradise ever since.

If salvation is by faith, who deceived you to believe you can earn it or lose it by your works?

This truth and this good news are worth dying for. Every other religion demands undertaking works, but our relationship with God is enjoyed by receiving. We are justified by the faith *of* the Son of God and that is the only thing capable of determining our eternal home. Only believe.

Now, if one belief can literally transform the eternal journey of our souls, then we should pay close attention to all our other beliefs, for in them, there is power to transform everything.

What is Truth Saying?

It only took a 2x2 photograph to get me interested and a twenty-minute conversation to fall in love with her. She was the girl of my dreams, fearfully and wonderfully made! I loved everything about her detailed design; long brown hair and big green eyes, compliments to her beautiful heart and fun loving spirit.

Unfortunately, my wife had struggled with bulimia for more than a decade. Every day for twelve years Satan spoke unkind words from the other side of the mirror to the woman I love. And, as the common story goes, she chose to believe and act in agreement with the lies concerning her God-created body.

Catherine had heard from someone else that she was not thin enough and these comments were received as value statements. Every time she looked into the mirror she saw imperfections; calves too big, skin too white, figure too fat. And, if being "fat" meant not being loved, then she had to take control and work hard to be lovable. My future wife's everyday schedule revolved around the gym, the bathroom and the measurements of calorie intake. Society's grotesque definition of beauty created an ungodly self-image that drove her to take thousands of pills to reshape her body. Her struggle to lose weight was a direct response to the lie that said, "You are not beautiful."

On the other hand, while flirting to the max, I spoke words of healing to my future wife: an onslaught of compliments about her voice, her smile and her legs delivered via poems, songs, emails and glances. This woman had to know that she was perfect, and I made it my personal mission to convince her. I only spoke of what I saw, the same words that I would have said whether she struggled with her self-image or not. I did not see myself as the truth that would rescue her, I was just ridiculously attracted and I loved sharing that fact. Her bulimia was not my focus, I was after her heart.

God had spoken words of love to her since before the foundations of the world, her parents have been speaking words of affirmation since the day of her birth, and I had been speaking words of encouragement since we met. And Catherine finally chose to reject the lies, and change what she believed.

A year after I met her we got engaged. Seven months later, we got married. Nine years after our wedding she looks more beautiful than ever, but now she believes it too and that enhances the truth. She made the decision to listen to God's truth, and the Truth set her free. She is now empowered by her testimony to speak life and freedom to others in self-hatred prisons. She heard the truth, agreed with it and now she is free indeed.

In the same manner, God is not focused on fixing our behavior, He is interested in winning our hearts. He knows that if we listen to Him and believe His value statements about our lives, bodies, past, present and future, then everything would change.

The problem is not what we hear, but what we believe. Freedom is not in people's words, but in our decision to receive the truth spoken over us. Somewhere along the line, a negative experience got us listening to the deceiver. Then a lie was spoken about us. This wicked information created an expectation that demanded a confirmation. Once the lie is confirmed, no matter what we do to challenge it, the only way to be free is to hear the truth and trust.

The father of lies has turned our minds into a battlefield for the soul. He intends to get you to agree with the lies he has spoken about your life; but there are two sides to the mirror of our existence. We either allow sin, Satan, circumstances, opinions and failures to determine who we are, or we listen to God. We get to choose the voice we shake hands with, and the one we call a liar.

The journey of breakthrough starts by recognition. The source of the lie is always the enemy of our souls, but we need to go back to the place where we signed the agreement to break it. We might have heard as a child:

> "It would have been better if you weren't even born." "You are stupid."

"I am so disappointed in you." "You will always be ____"

Those words provide an opportunity to believe them. Belief creates faith to see them through. And when our beliefs get reinforced by circumstances, those beliefs get fixed to our God given identity and begin to distort it.

The way out is looking in, or as the Bible says, "Be transformed by the renewing of your mind." [5] Our God who is able to restore the painful memories of our past, can speak truth into the deception that was established in our thoughts. His Spirit can then reveal the truth that will set us free:

"You were knitted in your mother's womb." "You have the mind of Christ."
"God is well pleased with you." "You will always be ___"

The questions our worship director, Amber Brooks, asked the first time she preached to our Sunday morning crowd were: "*Who told you were an addict? Who told you were worthless? Who told you were broken?*" God certainly didn't, someone else did.

Yes, Satan knows those labels might reflect real issues; behaviors you endure or words that have been spoken. What is most important to understand (and Satan knows this well) is that whatever you believe about yourself will determine the course of your career; whatever you believe about the opposite sex will influence how you treat your spouse; and whatever you believe about God will have an impact on how you pray and worship.

Stop eating from that tree and start pulling out those roots. Those labels do not define you! The Holy Spirit wants to guide you into all truth. He wants to expose anything that is not in line with God's word and loving character.

As it was declared to the church in Ephesus, "But God, being rich in mercy, **because of the great love with which he loved us**, even when we were dead in our trespasses, made us alive together with Christ—by grace you have been saved—and He has raised us up with him **and seated us with him in the heavenly places in Christ Jesus**." [6]

We are now seated on the very throne that Lucifer lusted after; the highest placement in the heavens, the seat of Christ Himself. We are in Christ Jesus, loved by God and full of the Holy Spirit. Satan's lies and deception could never get us there. Our efforts and good behavior will never lift us high enough. The only thing required is for us to listen to the correct voice, believe it fully and reject the falsehood we have accepted so far.

Disagreement with the enemy will get you into alignment with the Father. Transforming your thought life will reshape your outcome. Allowing the Spirit to highlight the lies will give you a road map for healing.

Let us take the opposite road Satan took, let us go for humility and surrender. Even compared to Eden, what we have now is far superior to the garden because the second Adam outdid the work of the first. We are now the apple of God's eye. We are the bride of Christ. We are the sanctuary of the Holy Spirit and according to the true Father, we are just right for loving.

Believe.

STUDY GUIDE: CHAPTER 5
THE OTHER "FATHER"

"Subsequently, if the role of a father is to give identity to the children, then Satan's main role is to give his false identity to his illegitimate sons and daughters."

Can you identify areas in your own life where you have believed lies about your identity that Satan, the father of lies, has whispered to you?

He comes to challenge our core identity, our sense of inner value and worth. When we look to the wrong places for these things, sinning is easy.

"What we believe is what we will become."

Sonship is natural when we believe we are God's sons.

"God is willing and able to change the doubts, the bitterness and the fear. But while God speaks truth to our hearts day by day, the enemy speaks lies to our minds constantly. And the way we manage our daily thoughts, determines which father we get our identity from."

It Starts with Belief!

*"Most of the un-godly emotions we experience originated
in a dirty lie we believed"*

There is a process to how we form beliefs,
- If you accept a belief, you reap a thought.
- If you sow a thought, you reap an attitude.
- If you sow an attitude, you reap an action.
- If you sow an action, you reap a habit.
- If you sow a habit, you reap a character.
- If you sow a character, you reap a destiny.

What you believe about yourself will ultimately determine your destiny.
We have to get to the root; to the place where we made the agreement.
If you don't know what that is look at the fruit and work backwards.

"The problem is not what we hear but what we believe."

CHAPTER SIX

REALLY GOOD NEWS

Gracious fathers lead their sons through the minefield of sin.
Indulgent fathers watch their sons wander off into the minefield.
Legal fathers chase them there. — DOUGLAS WILSON

Early in the morning, while Jesus spoke to a crowd in the temple, the Scribes and the Pharisees brought Him a woman who was caught in the act of adultery. Think about that. While she enjoyed the thrill of someone else's husband, she experienced the horror of being "found out." Then, she is dragged through the streets, probably half naked, with the smell of sweat, and tears, and dirty sex. She is brought to the temple and thrown at the feet of a perfect human; the only one who does not know how it feels to be caught doing wrong.

The Son of God was so near and she was so exposed. Imagine the shame, guilt, and regret; so many horrible feelings pounding at the door of her heart. Add to that, the awareness of the inevitable death by stoning, and it is safe to say, that she was having the worst day of her life.

The religious leaders were ready to go; anxious with stones in their hands, and the Law of Moses like a howl in their hearts. They were stimulated by the opportunity of proving their rectitude, and they saw this as a favorable moment to catch another "sinner" in his mistake, that glutton and drunkard from Nazareth. It was as if, the reflection of their own sin blinded them full of hate. There were no signs of leniency, and on this day, mercy was not an option.

Yet in the chaos of religious fervor, the story does not document that the woman begged for pity. There is no record of her asking forgiveness. She just stood there before Jesus, exposed and condemned. Suddenly, the Messiah got closer, kneeled down on the floor, and started to write on the ground. All eyes, including the woman who was standing alone in the circle, had to look down to see Jesus. He manifested with His body what He had already started to reveal through His word: He came down from heaven to save what was lost in the dirt. [1]

Finally, Jesus stands up and challenges the morning agenda, "Let him who is without sin among you be the first to throw a stone at her," and again, he bent down and wrote some more.

Perfect.

God the Son could not stand still in the presence of self-righteousness. He would not allow this woman to die as a payment for her sins. He knew that He was the only one capable of doing that effectively at the cross. Therefore His challenge and His conviction, made the men that brought her there, leave steadily, starting with the old men first. Everyone going their way, moving on with the weight of their own shame.

Meanwhile, the dirty lady remained in the temple of the Holy God, alone with Jesus. She was now with a different man who offered a different kind of intimacy. And this stranger who went down to the dirt and saved her from death asks, "Woman, where are they? Has no one condemned you?"

She can only state the obvious, "No one, Lord."

No one condemned her; no one threw a stone; not one of them. Jesus was the only one with the right to judge her anyways, but He chose not to. He did not even challenge her lifestyle, He did not correct her behavior or give her a 10-step program to sexual purity. What He did was much greater than the punishment she deserved; He extended His hand and welcomed her to live in grace.

Jesus said, "Go, and sin no more," as if to say, I went down to your level, now I welcome you up to mine. I will die your death and become your adultery. I will expose you without shame to my Father and all the good that belongs to me, will now belong to you.

The exposed sinner, standing before Jesus, was invited to the life that only the Son of God could live, a life of holiness and freedom. This woman did not pray the sinner's prayer, she did not memorize a bible verse or listen to any worship song. All she did was allow Jesus to save her and recognized Him as Lord. While everyone in town was conscious of her past sin, Jesus was conscious of her glorious future. Jesus believed that she could live that life, not because of her devout efforts or intentions of purity, but because of Him, her new, better lover.

This display of grace resonated in the hearts of the people that witnessed the event. The early church fathers were compelled to record this story in John 8, because there was something about that moment that had to be documented for the whole world to see. Because when

Jesus says, "Neither do I condemn you," He was repeating what He heard God the father saying. And when He said, "Go and sin no more," He was not saying it as false hope, He was summoning all of our hearts.

It could be summarized as this: "Go and live my life, in Me, through Me, and because of Me. And every time you get caught in the act of _____, I will forgive you before you ask, defend you with your accusers and embrace you again in the throne of grace."

For this reason we call it, Good News. Because this Jesus is not a religious leader; He is a Savior; and you can enjoy His extravagant love even right after you fall into your extravagant sin.

Sinners in the Hands of a Lovely God

If somehow you conclude that this story is grounds for living with permission to sin, then you have not yet seen the Holy King. He is righteous in all His ways, He is majestic and blazing white. No evil has ever been found in Him; He is forever honorable, just and pure. His name is Holy and He loves you way too much, to leave you in the dirt. He's too caring of a Father to not call out your transgression. He believes in you too much to see it all waste away in impurity, false religion, addiction, pornography, anger, gluttony, racism, gossip or fear. We are all, both the adulterous woman and the Pharisees, and we are in need of an encounter with salvation.

Sin is the biggest detractor for legitimate relationships. So we cannot move forward in our pursuit of relationship as sons of God and sons of men until we learn how to properly manage our internal struggles.

I can almost guarantee that, in the last twenty minutes, you *have* sinned. You offended God, you broke His law, and you failed at being perfect. Even if you just started to think, "Wait a second, I have done nothing sinful in the last twenty minutes?" I would like to remind you of James 4:17: "If anyone then knows the good they ought to do and doesn't do it, it is sin for them." So unless you just came back from feeding the hungry, washing the dishes no one told you to wash, or praying for the unreached people of western Africa, then yes, you have sinned. And now, thanks to this bit of writing, I have sinned myself! I have judged you for your immorality and I joined you in the company of the broken and defiled human race.

Actually, the Bible says that, "If we claim to be without sin, we deceive ourselves and the truth is not in us. If we confess our sins, he is faithful and just and will forgive us our sins and purify us from all unrighteousness."[2] There is only one who never sinned and only one who can deal with it the right way. That one, is neither you nor me, which based on the last paragraphs of admission, is very good news.

Jesus consumed our sexual impurity and our tendency to criticize others. At the cross, He endured our ungodly pride and became one with the sin that separates us from God. When the Father looked down and saw His Son bearing the sins of the world, He didn't see His Son, He saw our wickedness.

While Jesus died at the cross, the Father had to turn and look away. Not in anger toward his Son, but in wrath over the sin that sent Jesus to crucifixion. Although, God loved His Son as much as He ever had, at that moment, He turned away in revulsion towards the ugliness of sin. And, as the Father looked away, Jesus was forsaken.

We may not understand all the implications of Jesus' experience.

In fact, we would have to live through it ourselves to understand (no thanks). But, it was there on the cross that the Son of God completely identified with us sinners and died in our place. The only reason, the Father forsook His beloved Son, was because all of our sins were laid on Him. Christ died in our place—His enemies. God justly judged our sin through Him. Jesus became a curse and now in Him we are forgiven, holy, blameless, faithful, chosen and loved… and so much more.

Dealing with Sin, as a Non-Sinner

Here is how the sons and daughters of God deal with their sin: **they don't**. Jesus was tempted in every way, but never sinned. He lived as a perfect man, took His sinless life and gave it in exchange for everyone's sinful one. Jesus fully became sin for us, so that we could be the manifestation of the righteousness of God. The gospel is simple, yet so countercultural to our religious mindset.

For example: I don't like bananas, I love them! I eat two every day, always with a big glass of full fat chocolate milk. Every week, I get at least fifteen of them delivered to my door. But each one of those sweet bananas has no previous history with me. I was not involved in the planting process. I have no communication with the people who picked them. I just received them, have them as food items in my home, and finish their journey by consumption. By the end of the week every one of those bananas stops being an individual fruit and they unwillingly become, Carlos Alberto Rodríguez Sostre. All their nutrients, vitamins and fiber stop being part of the fruit and become part of me. Processed by my system, merged into my cells and expressed as my body. If you see me, you are actually seeing fifteen bananas.

Similarly, Jesus drank the cup of the wrath of God to the very last drop. He became one with the sin and the punishment that has been our meal since the beginning. He took from us, the fruit, all the depravity, guilt, fear and pain that we carried and consumed it. If you see Jesus, you are actually seeing every one of us.

At the same time, Jesus invited us to eat His body and drink His blood.[3] When Jesus shared this barbaric imagery in ancient Palestine it cost him a few disciples (and I kind of understand why) because it is madness to think that we must eat and drink another person to inherit eternal life! But that was Jesus' requirement. We feast on His flesh and we partake of His nature. We drink His blood and we absorb His perfection. We consume Him, the Tree of Life, and we receive His holiness, purity, character and faith.

Jesus humbled Himself, came and identified completely with you in your humanity, so that now you can be completely identified with Him in His divinity. — COLIN URQUHART [4]

"It is finished," cried the Son, as He became one with us, so that we would become one with Him. Yes, Jesus dealt fully and eternally with our sin. If we eat and drink Him, we have completely become one with Him. He had us for dinner at the cross; let us have Him for breakfast in resurrection.

Yet instead, when we try to sort out the problem of sin by ourselves, it implies that we don't believe the sacrifice was finished. But Jesus declared, "It is finished," at the top of His lungs and as the loudest shout eternity has heard. Since then, it *was* finished; it *has* been finished and it *will* continue to stay finished.

Sin has only one solution, and the solution: Jesus Christ, has already sorted out the problem. He paid the full price for everything we have done wrong. It is so complete, that even the sin that we will engage in tomorrow has already been redeemed. The only thing we can do about the incredible gift of grace is to accept it, then respond with surrender, with thanksgiving, and with worship.

It is in the acceptance of this truth, "We are one with Christ and we are one in the Father," [5] where we will be sanctified. Then we, as they always have, will triumph over sin. The joy and the pleasure now, is to manifest the holiness that already belongs to us, because of Him.

The Continual Struggle

Oops, you did it again! You had done so good at the confession, repentance and self-purification. You even passed through a complicated deliverance procedure and swore never to sin this way again. But this time, you did not just sin, you failed at staying pure, you broke the promises made to God and you regressed the process of sanctification. Oops indeed.

Everyday we seem to find multiple ways to do the wrong things over and over again. For some, it is lies and gossip. For a lot of people, it is sexual. It does not have to be an adulterous relationship, it could be the thought that transformed into a porn scene in our heads or the dirty website that found its way back into our lives. For the rest, it could be the pills, the cuts, or the finger down the throats again. And, to crown the list of offenses, most of us like to judge everybody else on their issues and their misbehaviors.

Nevertheless, we really want to stop. But, we confess, repent and purify, just to steal and hate and curse again. And, as the vicious cycle goes on, it all gets more entangled than the paragraph you just read.

Jesus declared, "You are already clean."[6] But how do we start to manifest that spiritual reality? When will that truth be seen as a fact in our life, here on earth? Yes, we *are* clean, but we want to *stay* clean!

While I gave a lecture at our School of Revival, a student asked me, "How do I stop? Just tell me how to stop sinning." The student's question gave me an opportunity to share, not on how to stop sinning, but on what to do after we sin.

Most of us have been taught, that after we sin, we need to react with repentance, which is a good idea. The problem is, that we have also been thought that repentance needs to last a long time, which is a (really) bad idea. The logic seems to be that the longer we torture ourselves with shame and regret, the better we will behave afterwards.

However, the word in Hebrew for repentance means "to change direction." Think about it, if you are walking down the road and suddenly realize that you are heading down a ditch full of nasty frogs that want to attack you like a plague, certainly you would turn in the opposite direction and run, as fast as you could.

Correspondingly, the word repentance in Greek means to "change your mind and leave the previous thought behind." Both the Greek and the Hebrew version of the same word imply an immediate reaction that changes the course of the journey and the thought process.

So how do we stop sinning? A good start is to change direction right after we fail. Satan's job is to point out our faults and celebrate how we missed the mark. Whenever we waste our time with feelings of shame and accusation, we might think we are speaking with God about our issues, but we are unknowingly talking with the enemy. If we are not careful, we could find ourselves kneeling before his accusatory finger instead of running towards the Father who already made a way for us to be free.

> "My little children, I am writing these things to you so that you may not sin. But if anyone does sin, we have an advocate with the Father, Jesus Christ the righteous. He is the propitiation for our sins, and not for ours only but also for the sins of the whole world."[7]

The best response, right after sin, is worship. We should react to our lack of holiness by setting our eyes on the one who is Holy, Holy, Holy. Right after we fall, we could go and worship Jesus, the one who never lied, cheated, or stole. Let's not give a second to the enemy to convince us that we are one with our sin. Let's run to the Father in repentance, where we can be reminded of our place as the beloved. On the other hand, when we find relief by feeling guilty, we expose the ungodly belief that we can beat sin on our own. But, you cannot beat sin my friend; so stop trying! Look to Jesus who already did. Return to the Father without hesitation, because when He sees you coming, He always sees Christ and He will always make a way for your deliverance.

Walking in the Light

God is light; in him there is no darkness at all. —1 JOHN 1:5

I went to a catholic school from kindergarten till fourth grade and I always remember how good the nuns were at getting me interested in the stories of David versus Goliath, Moses and the Red Sea, Jesus and the resurrection. I also remember the priest in his full attire, as he looked to the sky and spoke words that drew me in and made me think. But, what I most clearly recall is the imagery inside the building during weekly mass; the saints with un-moveable eyes that followed me as I walked in the chapel, and the thin, blood-stained figure of Jesus that made me feel sad for Him and everyone else.

At only eight years of age I was looking forward to my first visit to the confession booth. Without much knowledge of the process, the opportunity to finally get into the mystery box spoke to my young heart of the right thing to do. But, I never made it inside, life changed drastically for my mom that year and we started to visit a charismatic church, which revealed the same God, but in a different light.

Confession of sin is not an exclusive Catholic tradition; it is a New Testament instruction. The Scriptures describes confession as access to power, "Therefore, confess your sins to one another and pray for one another, that you may be healed. The prayer of a righteous person has great power as it is working." [8]

The worldly assumption is that confessing sin disempowers us by exposing our frailty, but it is the opposite. To *confess* means to openly declare, without reservation; to say it as it is, not holding back. It allows us to be healed or *iáomai*, a primitive verb that refers to a supernatural, physical or spiritual healing that brings attention to the Lord Himself.

When all the information we hold secretly in our hearts is out in the open, Satan has no way to keep us hostage and no bribe to control us with. Darkness loses its grip when our hidden sins are exposed. Just as a small swoosh of a match possesses the creative force to produce fire and empower the candle to produce more light, confession has the capacity to expose all the dark corners in our lives, rendering all the information useless for the enemy.

One thing is unavoidable, walking in sonship will require us to take relationships from a superficial level, to a depth that can only be found in light. "If we walk in the light, as he is in the light, we have fellowship with one another, and the blood of Jesus, his Son, purifies us from all sin." [9]

All that is required is a naked conversation; one that bypasses the formalities of hypocritical Christianity and sounds something like, "I have been dealing with this …" Then, we can give a two minute account of the sin we have been struggling with and trust God with our information. The spiritual parent who listens has two choices; reject you because of their misunderstanding of grace, or admire your willingness, your openness and your honesty. Either way, you win. Once your fault is out in the open then nothing from darkness can hinder your freedom. Walking in the light is a gift for the children.

Ready to try?

New Holy Expectation

There is a lie infiltrated in our generation that says, "We are condemned to a constant battle with sin." Yes, there are struggles and legitimate temptations. Yes, we are bombarded with the wrong values and incorrect expectations. Yes, there is pleasure to be found in sin; but the ultimate truth is that friendship with Jesus Christ the Son of God, is the greatest pleasure of all. When we set our eyes on Him, the author and perfecter of our faith, our walk of love is determined by our assurance of salvation, not our expectation of failure. It is a matter of focus and attention; for whatever has our attention, will get our affections.

Self-discipline is a fruit of the Spirit, [10] not a natural product of our own effort. It is a supernatural consequence of surrender to the Father, a direct outcome of being in His presence. Besides, part of the Lord's prayer says, "Free us from temptation and deliver us from evil." In that short portion of Scripture, God the Father made a commitment to go to battle for us against temptation and the evil ways. This is a crusade He already won through the sacrifice of the Son, we can receive it by faith as soon as we ask. Not only that, but He is *able to keep you from stumbling and to present you blameless before the presence of His glory with great joy."* [11]

His blood has never stopped washing away your sin and His heart has never changed His opinion about you. We are truly set up to be more than conquerors.

Finally, according to the Revelation that John saw in the island of Patmos, "They will make war on the Lamb, and the Lamb will conquer them, for he is Lord of lords and King of kings, and those with Him are *called and chosen and faithful.*" [12]

You see that? The ultimate King and Lord wins the war, and His people inherit the benefits and titles. So today, when you look at yourself in the mirror, eliminate the grumpy hope that you will struggle with sin again. Agree with God and declare the announcement heaven is shouting over you: *called, chosen and faithful.* Jesus is coming back for a pure and spotless bride and that is exactly how the Father sees you and me.

However, in case you do end up struggling with sin and temptation, start to worship, quickly change direction and remain exposed to the Father of lights. And never forget, if the Son sets you free, you are free indeed.

Read John 8:1–11.

How do you respond when you hear the story of the women caught in adultery and hear that "You can enjoy His extravagant love even after you fall into your extravagant sin?"

How do you respond to his gift of grace in Jesus' death on the cross?
Do you struggle to receive that truth of grace?

What is your usual response to sin?
To hide from God, to live in guilt and shame, or to confess? How do you feel about Carlos' suggestion of how we respond to sin—to worship and run to him? Can you identify mindsets that you have which would need to change in order for you to respond in worship?

Walking in the Light

Do you have relationships where you can freely confess your sin and receive acceptance?

Accountability

"Therefore confess your sins to each other and pray
for each other so that you may be healed. The prayer
of a righteous person is powerful and effective."

— JAMES 5:16

Being accountable means:

> The quality or state of being accountable; especially: an
> obligation or willingness to accept responsibility or to
> account for one's actions.

Are there people in your life that you can ask to hold you accountable?
People who will ask you the hard questions. People who you can confess
your sins to, receive acceptance and love, but who will also challenge
you and support you in living differently.

CHAPTER SEVEN

THE HAPPY NUMBER 2

A godly leader finds strength by realizing his weakness,
finds authority by being under authority,
finds direction by laying down his own plans,
finds vision by seeing the needs of others,
finds credibility by being an example,
finds loyalty by expressing compassion,
finds honor by being faithful,
finds greatness by being a servant.

— ROY LESSIN

The story of Joshua should be our story. He was courageous, determined and reliant on God's direction. He was the commander in the very first combat Israel was involved in after their departure from Egypt.

He responded to the doubt of other leaders with extravagant faith, and was more loyal to Moses than any other man during the journey through the desert. Two individuals, from a whole generation, were allowed to enter into the promised land and Joshua was one of them. He was also one of the two men allowed to approach the mountain where God manifested His presence in its entire splendor and he was the only one involved in every story of the Exodus.

Yet, when the author of the book of Joshua decided to define his identity, he did not choose the words *leader* or *commander, champion* or *prophet*. Not even the meaning of his name—*Jehovah my help*—would be the specification used. In the first verse of the book that carries his first name, his identity is revealed as "Joshua the son of Nun, Moses' assistant."

> "After the death of Moses the servant of the LORD,
> the LORD said to Joshua the son of Nun, Moses' assistant,
> 'Moses my servant is dead.'" [1]

What a start! Joshua's moment to shine had arrived, out of the shadow of his predecessor. It was now his turn to take the people of God into their next season of conquest. Still he has to hear it again, *Moses is the servant of the Lord*. The supreme title did not pass on to him, it was reserved for his spiritual father.

Could it be possible that even after being faithful all the way from Egypt up to this moment, God himself would still be raving about Moses; the guy who got angry and was forbidden to enter into the land that flows with milk and honey?

I know Moses was an epic man of God but we have got to give

Joshua some credit here, cut him some slack. After all, this is chapter one, verse one, of the book titled under *his* name.

What's more, Moses' actual name had not been mentioned as much in one chapter of the previous five books as it is in the first chapter of the book of Joshua.

> "Moses my servant is dead; now therefore arise" v2
> "As I said unto Moses" v3
> "As I was with Moses" v5
> "Which Moses my servant commanded you" v7

This is no other than God himself speaking to Joshua. It is the first, direct encounter between the God of Israel and the new leader of His people. This is the perfect opportunity for the Lord to establish credibility, speak identity and make Joshua feel confident about his new role. But if this was a test of humility and character, a battle for the heart of Joshua to remember his origins, then the new leader passed with flying colors.

These verses now are Joshua speaking:

> "Remember the word that Moses the servant of the Lord
> commanded you" v13
> "In the land that Moses gave you" v14
> "The land that Moses the servant of the Lord gave you" v15

He acknowledged God's divine road of inheritance. He understood that his service to Moses empowered him to be in this new position of leadership—not as the servant of the Lord himself, but as Moses' assistant.

It was Joshua who went ahead in battle, when Moses gave the order. He was the man disposed to follow Moses up the terrible mountain. He was the one whose name was changed from *Hoshea* to Joshua by the revelation of Moses. And he was the one who remained close to the tent to enjoy the glory that visited Moses. Joshua was the man who left a life of slavery in Egypt and voluntarily became a servant to the man whom God chose for deliverance.

And Joshua is a type of Christ. He was the leader who came not for himself, but was sent by the Father to bring his children into the promised land. Yet as a leader, as a champion and as the Son, Jesus is also *the servant of God*.[2] In the same manner, He is a servant to us; for *"I am among you as the one who serves."*[3] **The only thing Jesus never served was His own agenda**. For us then, receiving the power of servant leadership might require a certain amount of death to our own pursuit of titles and positions—in fact, total death! This really should be our story.

And what if this *is* your destiny? What if *servant* is your main title? How would you handle the knowledge that you might live and die under someone else's shadow?

Next time you read the exploits of Joshua, remember that He was *not* the servant of the Lord; Moses was. Joshua just followed the leader and became—for the Israelites—a manifestation of the promises Moses received in the mountain. Next time you worship Jesus as the King of Kings and Lord of Lords, remember that He was given those titles by His Eternal Father. He did not come to earn them, they are the byproduct of the greatest servant's heart.

Joshua was a happy number two. Jesus is a happy number two. Are you?

The Day I Died

Immediately after we walked in the door we heard the worship, felt God's presence and knew that we were home. Catherine and I were on our first year of marriage and had found this community, Pabellón de la Victoria in Camuy, Puerto Rico, through a mutual friend. On the first day, Pastor "Tito" Cabán and his wife Sandra welcomed us in and, as soon as we hugged, we connected deeply.

We went from visiting for the first time, to hanging out every weekend, to becoming their youth pastors, in less than four months. This incredible couple made a way for us, not just to be leaders in their house, but also to be family with them.

That first Sunday we arrived, they were just sending out the last remnant of leaders who were not in agreement with their love for the move of the Spirit. Tito and Sandra had chosen the river of God's presence above all else, and some of their dear friends who had walked the road with them in the past, chose to move on.

Catherine and I arrived in a difficult but exciting time of transition for the church. God took us on a journey of growth that still bears good fruit in our lives today. We preached the Father's love message every chance we got. We continually ministered heart healing to the leaders and the congregation. We started to reach to the poorest of the poor in the city, and began to see signs and wonders in all of our meetings. We wrote songs, recorded a worship album, and brought in some of the most anointed people on the planet to share at the local church. Tito and Sandra were beyond humble and teachable. They made room for our gifting and we made room in our lives for theirs. And it was their leadership and passion for Jesus that made way for a legitimate move of God that is still ongoing today.

However, after three years of incredible love and unity, I was convinced that all these good things were happening in the church because of me. I was deceived to the core and I found myself regularly annoyed on Sunday mornings. I could hear my thoughts as I criticized everything done by the rest of the leadership: "the offering talk is too long; we are not doing enough Father Heart ministry; this worship is not going anywhere." And on and on my pride spoke.

Tito preached deep, fresh and challenging messages, but I could not see the good in it. There were miracles happening in his ministry time that I had never seen before in mine. Somehow it felt like he was stealing and then twisting my revelations and doing much better than I was.

I started to believe that something was wrong and someone needed to correct it. "He just needs a bit more heart healing" I thought; "We are not focusing on the right things; they should be doing this, and that, or the other." My pride kept whispering in my ear and polluting my already broken heart.

One morning, I laid on the cold tile floors of our church after having this thought: "Wow, today they are striving so much that I'm going to have to show them how to rest in His presence." My statement sounded spiritual but it was full of jealousy and contempt.

The truth is that the Father is more interested in our hearts than our ministries. He cares more about our character and integrity than He does about our anointing or calling, but it is amazing how ministry and the anointing can provide the perfect scenario for our true character to be revealed and our hearts to be healed.

Therefore, as I lay there pretending to be right, I had a picture of the Trinity walking by. The Father, the Son and the Holy Spirit drew near to me from the East and the West. This was literally a holy ambush! I saw the Father as he sat on the ground and placed His hands on my chest. The Son sat just above my head and started stroking my hair. The Holy Spirit was moving all around me, with fire, wind and glory.

Just then I realized that God had come close to love me out of pride and into life. "Why am I even here? These people don't receive my message anymore, why won't you just give me my own church to lead?" I said—straight into honesty, by-passing the religious chatter and sharing exactly what I felt. I was angry and frustrated. Things were not going my way. In my eyes, people did not value my call or my message anymore. Somehow, God needed to understand that Tito was wrong, and I was right.

Tears of disappointment started to well up as I shared with God my complaint. The Father listened, Jesus cared and the Holy Spirit was attentive as I shared. Then, because of His loving kindness, God asked me the most revealing of questions, "What if I asked you to be number two to Tito for the rest of your life?"

Ouch! The question asked proved that this was really God speaking for I would have never put myself in that predicament. Only He could be so fatherly and yet so challenging.

> *My son, do not regard lightly the discipline of the Lord,*
> *nor be weary when reproved by him. For the Lord disciplines the*
> *one he loves, and chastises every son whom he receives.*
> — HEBREWS 12:6-10 (ESV)

By this point I was aware that I would not get away with anything else but dying to that immaturity and pride. There was no getting up from the floor without surrendering, not just to God but also to serving my fellow man.

Afterwards, Jesus leaned over to me and while He looked straight into His Father's eyes, He said, "I love being second place." My heart broke because I knew what they were asking; they wanted me to be Joshua but my hunger was to be Moses; they wanted me to serve, but my passion was to lead.

Since getting involved in church I had always desired to be in ministry: epic hopes for the work of God. The problem was that the goal turned into ambition for leadership and the ambition turned into the pride that contaminated my heart.

So the Father asked again, "Are you willing? My Son has been my willing number two for all of eternity. Will you join Him?"

For thirty seconds I went into defense mode. I felt attacked and fearful about losing my dreams. I tried to explain to myself the theological reasons why that language was not right. I wanted to escape this moment and disregard it as false humility being produced by my imagination. Then, I tried to remember all the prophetic words spoken about my calling, the missions, church planting and crusades. "How could I ever do these as a number two?"

"No, Father," I said through bitter tears, "I don't think I can." Then I paused, as I heard my own voice, for it sounded like an orphan who begs to belong. I knew I was wrong, and I knew this was sin. So I took a deep breath and I felt God's kindness surround me. There I was, contradicting God, holding on to ambition and trying hard not to die but He still loved me while showing me compassion in my weakness.

The best I could do was to rebuild my answer. "I don't feel like I am prepared God, but I want to be. Teach me to be a number two."

And the Trinity smiled.

Immediately, Jesus leaned over to me one more time and said: "You will *love* being number two."

When my soul heard the sound of His voice, everything stopped. His statement was like a whisper that initiated a tornado. I felt as if my heart got ripped from the inside out, and in one moment, I was changed forever.

I was properly sobbing and trying as hard as I could, to say out loud, "I am willing Father, make me a number two."

After twenty minutes of crying out the pain and receiving the joy of surrender, I got up and everything looked different. Worship sounded heavenly and Tito's sermon went straight into my spirit. There were no walls between us and I left the room more alive than ever. From that moment on, I was convinced wholeheartedly that if God asked me to be number two to this man for the rest of my life, I would love it.

Success?

This new reality had nothing to do with any self manufactured humility. This was an invitation for true honor and it came as a gift from God to my heart. This Jesus who invited me to be number two was the same one who said to His disciples, "But whoever would be great among you must be your servant, and whoever would be first among you must be slave of all." Multiple times in the gospels we can read as the disciples discuss their entitled placement of honor. This thirst for position in them seemed not just to be worldly ambition, but learned behavior. We see it as the mother of James and John falls at the feet of Jesus to beg Him for a throne for her boys. This of course causes the others to become indignant at the request. The other ten were not offended at the lack of maturity in the "mama's boys". What they were concerned with was the possibility of those two thrones not being available for them. Yet Jesus did not deny their pursuit of greatness, He only redirected it to the proper trail.

The one true King had to continually teach these men servant leadership. "For even the Son of Man came not to be served but to serve, and to give his life as a ransom for many." [5] Jesus did not come to establish leaders that would rule over society, churches or each other; He came to rescue sinners, reveal the Father and invite them to serve one another. His method was not based on the old model of leadership. Jesus washed their feet, gave His life and still serves us today by interceding to the Father.

There was always a constant pressure on Jesus from His followers to give them power for the sake of power and not for the sake of others. We see this pattern in every nation, in every denomination and in every people group, but good intentions in orphan hearts have become genocides all over the world. Young men in their efforts to bring change have become mass murderers or "successful" dictators. The desire for public service is turned into corruptive works. Too many leaders who started out with the right motivations, have ended up on the wrong side of the table. The spirits of religion and politics have polluted the heart of well intended people and created an army of deceivers who rule through injustice and fraud.

The problem is not that it *can* happen to anybody, but that it *has* happened to too many. Power and pride are a deadly combination. When we are unable to recognize the innate human thirst for power within us, we are easily tricked to believe that our pursuit of supremacy is virtuous. We can constantly work to be the king, but we will only end up as a slave with a throne.

The formula for success in Heaven is the opposite of the formula for success on earth. I guess that is the reason why Jesus played the cards backwards. He left the throne to become a servant, and died a servant's death.

No one could say it better than Paul in his letter to the Philippians, "Agree with each other, love each other, be deep-spirited friends. Don't push your way to the front; don't sweet-talk your way to the top. Put yourself aside, and help others get ahead. Don't be obsessed with getting your own advantage. Forget yourselves long enough to lend a helping hand. *Think of yourselves the way Christ Jesus thought of himself.* He had equal status with God but didn't think so much of himself that he had to cling to the advantages of that status no matter what. Not at all. When the time came, he set aside the privileges of deity and took on the status of a slave, and became human! Having become human, he stayed human. It was an incredibly humbling process. He didn't claim special privileges. Instead, He lived a selfless, obedient life and then died a selfless, obedient death-and the worst kind of death at that: a crucifixion."[6]

The great men and women of this world are usually the ones that move from the burden of "this is good for me" to the pleasure of "this will be good for them." What if instead of seeing our boss as the unbearable number one, we saw ourselves as a happy number two?

What if, instead of demanding to be treated as the number one at home, we saw ourselves as a joyful number two to our family? What if instead of being the number one critic of our pastor, we become an enthusiastic number two, at their service. Anyone who wants to be first must be the very last, and the servant of all.

So go ahead sons and daughters. Show off your silver medal. It was never God's design for anyone to be on the very top. That place belongs only to Him. Let His knees be your throne, let His kindness be your language, and let His power be your glory. Besides, when your identity is sonship, your title will truly be *servant*.

THE HAPPY NUMBER 2

"When your identity is sonship you title will truly be servant."

What if servant was your main title?
How would you handle the knowledge that you might live and die under someone else's shadow?

Are you a happy number two?
What areas of your life would look different if you approached them as a happy servant rather than seeking your own gain or agenda?

CHAPTER EIGHT

WHOSE SON ARE YOU?

The saddest thing about being fatherless is that
you don't have a father to honor. — TRACEY ARMSTRONG

In our father-hungry generation where one of the main struggles is comparison, it would be unfair to find a son who is talented, good looking and anointed. The rest of us cope with knowing that we can barely get one of the three. However, there is a man in the Bible who was all of that, and then some. The name of this specimen was David. If his remarkable nature wasn't enough, he was also made the king of Israel without even trying. A man after God's own heart.

The stories related to "David The Beloved" spoke about a capable shepherd trusted with the care of hundreds of sheep; a valiant sentinel, who would have killed bears and lions to protect the assets of his father. Saul, the king of Israel, knew David for his skills as a songwriter and artisan of musical instruments. The Bibles says he could produce sounds with his harp that forced evil spirits to depart from Saul yet his family used to call him "the little one" and as such, they would treat him. In spite of this, history will always remember him as the boy who killed the giant.

When Israel was at war with the Philistines, King Saul was faced with one of the hardest decision of his rule. He had to choose a warrior who would fight the giant named Goliath, and let that sole man bear the burden of bringing victory to Israel. One would assume that out of a nation of millions, a really tall guy with battle skills and unparalleled faith on God's assistance would arise. Why not? That was the history of Israel: the nation goes to battle, *Yahweh* wins the war.

However, for forty days they waited and no one stepped up to face the huge Philistine challenge. Not even the King himself stepped forward. He *was* the tallest and strongest of all the men in the land. He was the man with the prophetic word, the title and the supernatural backing of Heaven; the one chosen by God, anointed by Samuel and crowned as the first monarch of Israel.

King Saul missed the opportunity to lead by example, the only legitimate way to be a leader besides dictatorship. Instead, he made a really bad military decision and selected a young shepherd who was untrained in the art of war and disregarded by his own family. Saul sends the boy he knew as a musician to face the giant warrior he was meant to fight himself.

David went ahead, charging into combat without Saul's armor. The boy ran with a battle cry that was louder than all the voices in the frontline. "The Lord who delivered me from the paw of the lion and from the paw of the bear will deliver me from the hand of this Philistine." [1]

But then, the Bible recollects a most interesting and overlooked part of this famous story:

> "As soon as Saul saw David go out against the Philistine, he said to Abner, the commander of the army, 'Abner, *whose son is this youth?*' And Abner said, 'As your soul lives, O king, I do not know.' And the king said, 'Inquire whose son the boy is.' And as soon as David returned from the striking down of the Philistine, Abner took him, and brought him before Saul with the head of the Philistine in his hand. Saul said to him, 'Whose son are you young man?' And David answered, 'I am the son of your servant Jesse the Bethlehemite.'" [2]

Saul sat on his throne under a special tent designed for royalty. He was served by peasants and counseled by the wisest minds. From there he watches the combat, as David slings the rock, swings the sword, and the tide of fear turns from the camp of Israel to the camp of the Philistines. The little one caused a shift in the atmosphere; a transfer of courage. Fear was no longer being breathed in by the Israelites but the boldness of the young, good-looking shepherd became the faith of a whole army.

Within the madness of victory, King Saul needed to know just one thing. There was one piece of information that would explain this series of events. The King does not want to know how much David prayed or which songs he wrote; he's not worried about his calling or his prophetic words. There were no congratulations or protocol of gratitude. As the boy returned to the tent dragging the head of Goliath in his hand,

Saul, like a desperate man, is searching for the most important answer. He asks David, "Whose son are you, young man?"

The king needed to know who the father of the boy was, acting in the way he himself should have acted all along. In Saul's reasoning, the only thing that could explain why this boy was so brave, believed the way he did, and fought when no one else would, had to be related to his father. It had to be! Weak men cannot reproduce giant slayer; cowards could never raise a valiant warrior. This son who is carrying the nation on his shoulders was the evidence of a courageous father.

Then, as the ground still rumbles and Israel's army plunders the Philistines, David shakes with adrenaline, smiles with hope, and gives a simple answer to the king: "I am the son of your servant Jesse the Bethlehemite."

King Saul's inquiry about David's biological father is one of the most revealing questions in the Bible. If I want to know your faith, I need to meet you father, yet we are constantly running away from that identification. We refuse to believe that we are able to do what we do because of who our father is. We wish it could be the other way around, that we have made men of ourselves and our abilities have been learned, not taught. Sometimes it seems as if we are determined to prove how orphan we are.

But! Identity is deposited, authority is delegated, and courage is learned. The good news is that your true Father is in fact the commander of the angel armies and in consequence you were destined for success, glory and victory. If you truly are a child of God, then your victories are not a by-product of your efforts but a direct link to your sonship. The boldness that David displayed in the battlefield was the fruit of faith, nurtured through the root of worship. He knew what God was capable of, not just because he had killed lions and bears in the past, but because he had looked into the heart of God in adoration and found favor in the Father's delight.

God His Father

Ethan the Levite, a psalmist and leader in the nation, had a revelation of the relationship between God and David. Psalm 89 was written as a tribute to that relationship and as a summons to make that connection our own and not just David's. Look to the earthly king who relied on the heavenly King, the earthly warrior who depended on the heavenly Savior, the earthly son who would call out: "You are my Father, my God, and the Rock of my salvation." [3]

David had deep revelation of God's fatherly ways: "As a father has compassion on his children, so the LORD has compassion on those who fear him." [4] He knew of God's protection and wrote intimate songs about His love. "The Beloved" was a man full of desire for God's presence and he even made a way for others to encounter grace. This child walked in a revelation that was ahead of his time as he acted like a worshipper who lived in the new covenant. He spoke to God as a friend not just a servant. He expected forgiveness when he repented of his sin, he trusted the Father with his earthly throne and was given one for eternity.

His closeness and relationship with God not only affected David but it affected God Himself, for it was David who chose Jerusalem to be the capital of the kingdom of Israel. Like a father who loves to please his kids about where to live, God saw that it was good. It is also on the throne of David that Jesus will sit forever giving honor to the man who ruled the kingdom as a son himself. [5] This singer-turned-shepherd-turned-king had a special understanding of what is available for those who walk in sonship towards God. David's expectation from his reality of being abandoned by his earthly fathers was that God Himself would be a "A father to the fatherless, a defender of widows, that's God in His holy dwelling." [6]

We celebrate David the man who wanted to build a house for the Lord but it was really God who wanted to build a house for David. The deep connection between David and God still baffles preachers and theologians all over the world. Based on the accounts of his sins and moral failures there is no reason for the Father to treat this man as his favorite. Yet favorite he is, not because God *has* favorites, but because some people just live like they are and that makes all the difference.

Jesse His Father

We can agree that there is something peculiar about the way Jesse treated David. The evidence lies in the biblical text. The prophet Samuel had a revelation from God to bring all the sons of Jesse together and see then who would be anointed king of Israel. After seeing the first seven sons, Samuel was forced to ask the question, "Are these all your sons?" By not having David with them inside the house, Jesse sent a message to his family and to David. No wonder his brothers seemed to dislike the little one, it appears to be the standard set by the father.

Nonetheless, even when rejection knocked at the door of his heart, David responded with mercy. He never denied his place in his earthly father's house. In addition, David is known multiple times throughout the story of his life as "the son of Jesse." This is not a title he denies or tries to correct. As we saw in the account after the battle with Goliath, David's answer to the question of the king was simply "The son of your servant Jesse." He carried the name of his household and he esteemed it in high regard even before royalty.

Then, while being persecuted by King Saul, David made a request to the King of Moab to protect the life of his father Jesse.[7] He lived as a man grateful for what he did receive under the tutelage of Jesse. He did the same with King Saul and it became the perfect example of how to deal with father figures who are unreachable, beyond redemption and absolutely crazy.

But the key to David's success in life was the connection with his other Father. Even when David seemed to be rejected out of his house, out in the field, he connected with God as dad.

Psalm 23 speaks from what appears to be a season of rejection from Jesse the father. But to the son David, it became the place of uncovering the goodness of the Lord Shepherd. All things worked together for the good of this beloved.

Saul His Father-In-Law

And some told me to kill you, but I spared you. I said, "I will not put out my hand against my lord, for he is the Lord's anointed."

*See, **my father**, see the corner of your robe in my hand. For by the*
fact that I cut off the corner of your robe and did not kill you, you
may know and see that there is no wrong or treason in my hands. I
have not sinned against you, though you hunt my life to take it.

— 1 SAMUEL 24:10-11 (ESV)

Jealousy turned into rejection, and rejection into a full scale manhunt.
The worshipper who had played the harp and freed Saul from evil
spirits, the shepherd who defeated the giant and gave the King his
greatest victory, the young man who married his daughter and became
a brother to his son, now hides in a cave to save his life. How could
Saul despise David with this full-on throw-javelins-at-your-head kind of
hatred? The mad king wanted nothing more than to annihilate David
when his son-in-law wanted nothing more than to honor him.

In the classic book, *A Tale of Three Kings*, author Gene Edwards
wrote, "How do you know when it is finally time to leave the Lord's
anointed? David never made the decision. The Lord's anointed made
it for him. The king's own decree settled the matter! 'Hunt him down;
kill him like a dog.' Only then did David leave, and he left alone."

Somehow, through this odyssey of pain, David managed to view
Saul as a father who warranted honor and allegiance. We read in
Samuel 24 that he had an opportunity to end the madness by killing
the first king, and the people would have been glad to be free from his
dictatorship. Most of Saul's soldiers would have happily joined the ranks
of David the giant slayer. Thousands of people would have received him
with songs of joy as he entered the city gates. The prophets would smile
at the fulfillment of Samuel's prophecy and a fresh spring would arrive.

Some had encouraged David to get rid of the king. Good friends who had given him good counsel in the past asked David to finish this season of pain, but David made the right call. He preserved the King's life and in turn, preserved his heart. Against all of the human longing for judgment, the one who was chosen by God decided to honor the one who had been rejected by God.

Just like David, it is in the cave of rejection that we make the important choices. It is in that place where fairness takes a back seat to loyalty. By deciding not to lift our hands, our words, or our pride against the Lord's anointed we position ourselves to hear the new psalms of deliverance. David manifested honor to the spiritual father God had chosen for him. Saul was the authority over the land David lived in; he was the ruler over the throne David would inherit, he was the father of David's wife, and this man, despite his lunacy, deserved respect.

> *No trumpets sound when the important*
> *decisions of our life are made.*
> *Destiny is made known silently.*
> — AGNES DE MILLE

My (and Your) Father

"Whose son are you?" This is the question that has always challenged my heart. After years of being part of the revival in Toronto where I received the favor of amazing men and women of God, I found myself sitting in a tent, full of promises, titles and prophetic words, but provoked by fear, shame and the inability to respond.

It was 2004, and after more than three years of enjoying the river that flowed constantly at the Toronto Airport Christian Fellowship, I was back home in the desert valley of the past. I was living with my parents, disconnected from my home church and with zero invitations to share the message that burned inside of me. Nobody cared that I had been John Arnott's intern. Nobody wanted to hear about my trips to Indonesia, Ukraine, or Kenya. There was no interest to learn about the miracles, signs and wonders that forever ruined my life for God.

I was back home and I felt like a nobody. Even though I had shared the message of God's love and knew theologically that my identity did not rely on what I did, I felt unloved and insignificant. The message of the Father's love that I preached became just relevant information with an expiration date; useless for my present state.

It was as if I had never truly heard the message. I felt like I was not a son. I felt unloved, not chosen. For days and weeks and months I waited to feel what I had felt in Toronto. I wanted the experience of God's embrace, I wanted the approval of men and the honor of my leaders but today, I can honestly say, I am glad I did not get it.

With tears in my eyes I would bring my complaint to God and through clenched teeth I would ask: "Where are you now? How come I don't feel anything? Where are my friends, my pastors, my church, my family?" Over and over again, within the toxic mix of anger, disappointment, confusion, and doubt, God would reply with a question of his own:

> "Are you still my son? When no one's looking, when no one responds to your sermons, when no one gets healed

through your prayers, when no one is speaking life or encouraging your destiny? Carlos, whose son are you?"

I had to learn through that season that my identity was not dependent on my works, but totally on God's acceptance. The information on the Father's love that had revolutionized my life started to become revelation that healed my heart. "No matter who is looking Father, I am still your boy. I'm Carlos Alberto the son of God the Father."

Then, I accepted my place in my earthly father's house. I stopped the fight against my own family and I began to honor from my heart. I began to feel God's comfort and that led me to be comfortable in the season I was living in.

It was in the place of "not being wanted" that I discovered God's passion for me. Not my doings, not my sermons, not even my good behavior … just me.

Our desire as children of God should be to seek a history that has been healed, an identity that has been sealed, and a destiny that has been revealed. In knowing our fathers we truly know our sonship, and in knowing our sonship we can truly reign as his kings and queens.

In David's life the fruit of walking in sonship to God as father and leader, was this: He became the second King of the United Kingdom of Israel. He became a ruler and strategist who brought fame, power and provision to his people. For multiple years he was able to achieve peace, and increase the wealth in the land. He brought back God's manifest presence in the ark, and made a way for the greatest house of worship this broken earth has ever seen built.

David failed morally, abused his powers and broke covenant with God. But for some reason, even when his sins looked worse than many others in scripture, God kept a special place for him. He paid a heavy price for those iniquities, but they did not disqualify his sonship. That was who he was, not what he was trying to be. "Son" is what he understood of himself.

And this Beloved knew the answer to the King's question. He was a son of the God of compassion. He was the son of Jesse from Bethlehem who trained him as a shepherd. And he was the son of Saul, the king who blessed him to rule. [8]

David also became a great father, which is the true sign of a good son. He led his son Solomon to be greater than him, and in turn, Solomon became a true father himself. He wrote the books of Proverbs and Ecclesiastes, not as a list of things we should try hard to do wisely, but as an invitation to his sons to live godly lives. It is a collection of his journey (which was full of mistakes) with opportunities to learn from a father to a son. Now, these became the Words of God himself, the wisest father of them all. Be the son who has nothing better to give, than a reply to this question: "Whose son are you?"

Your greatness is hidden in the answer.

STUDY GUIDE: CHAPTER 8
WHOSE SON ARE YOU?

Read 1 Samuel 17–31. David's victory in battle was a direct result of the fact that he knew his identity as a son. He knew that God would come through for him.

Is this revelation making its way to your heart?

> *"If you truly are a child of God, then your victories are not a by-product of your efforts but a direct link to your sonship."*

Carlos shares his journey of life back at home after his season in Toronto.

Have you come to a place of accepting the truth of your identity as a child of your Heavenly Father?

Do you know in your heart that his acceptance of you is not dependent on the works that you do for him, or how long you pray and read the Bible?

Here we learn a process to walk with God. To seek a history that is healed, an identity that is sealed, and a destiny that has been revealed. **Can you identify where you and the Father are in this journey?**

We manifest sonship by honouring the fathers and mothers that God has placed in our lives. David chose to honour his spiritual father despite being treated unfairly by Saul. David submitted himself to his authority.

What is the state of your heart toward both your earthly parents and spiritual?

Are you living with the heart of a son towards them? If not, what do you need to do to make this right?

CHAPTER NINE

SONSHIP TO YOUR OWN

It is wise for a father to know his child.
But it is wiser for a child to take the time to know his father.

— ANONYMOUS

Although the Israelites were captives to the Roman Empire they still celebrated their freedom from the oppression of Egypt. Because of it, Jesus traveled every year with his family to partake of the bread, the wine and the music of the Passover festival. It took five days to walk from Nazareth to Jerusalem, but it had to be done for this was the ultimate spiritual vacation.

At the end of the long journey, just before you entered the great city, there was still a reminder of Roman tyranny. All the tourists could see the lawbreakers who were being executed on the hills outside of the city. The preferred method used was crucifixion, and it was only reserved for slaves, revolutionaries and vile criminals. One day soon, the boy considered, it had been reserved for Him.

Once Jesus entered the gates, thousands of people could be heard singing the name of *Yahweh*, their deliverer. The symbolism of the feast resonated inside the young heart of Jesus as it spoke of the blood sacrifice that was required for redemption. The feast reminded Him of the Scriptures that Mary read to Him before bedtime. It gave imagery to the stories that Joseph shared with Him as they worked together in the wood shop. It burned in His heart as a love song for His Father and as a cry of hope for the salvation of His people.

At twelve years old the atmosphere of remembrance allowed Jesus to have the awakening of an internal confession. As in an open vision, the festival gave Him a glimpse of His destiny. It was an intimate encounter with the ancient prophecies that spoke about Him. He saw the messianic promise and understood Himself to be the lamb that would be slain for the sins of the world, not just the iniquities of the Jewish people who celebrated, but also for the transgressions of the Romans who oppressed.

The Son of Man was soon to be manifest as the Messiah, the Savior and the greatest Rabbi. The one with the mission to reveal the Father to these people. And it became clear to Him that year.

This discovery made Him feel like He belonged in the temple. Not with his family on the journey back, but with the priests, the Levites and the teachers of the law. Between the sinners crucified and the Passover lamb sacrificed, the boy Jesus was compelled to remain in the city.

While His voice still cracked in the process of puberty, and His body tumbled through teenage growth, He concluded:

"This is my Father's house, this is my Father's business."

He then did something Mary and Joseph were not accustomed to. When the festival was done, Jesus stayed back in Jerusalem in what appeared to be His first act of disobedience. They expected maturity and wisdom from their son, for they only knew Him as one who manifested absolute obedience. So mom and dad spent more than a day assuming He was around, walking back alongside their relatives. They had no previous experience that would have said to them, "Warning! Warning! If you have not seen Jesus in the last thirty minutes something bad must have happened," (which is the expectation of most parents on a road-trip with their kids).

I can imagine Mary saying, "Don't worry Joseph, he must be in the back helping grandma walk," while Joseph replies, "I'm not worried honey, I'm sure he's helping the neighbors fix their cart, you know how he is."

It was after 24 hours of travel that mom and dad finally realized that they had lost God![1] The special Son, who was given by the Holy Spirit, protected from Herod's death squads and faithful to fix his bed every morning, was nowhere to be found!

The story in Luke 2 is so normal and human that it is easy to imagine these parents freaking out. As any other guardian would, Mary and Joseph spent morning, afternoon and evening searching for their first-born. No cell phone, Facebook or Twitter to help in the quest, only a sea of people with endless (negative) possibilities. On this occasion, there was no angel to give Joseph a dream and there was no angel Gabriel leading Mary to find the Messiah, so they desperately searched for three long days.

Then on the fourth day they found Him in the temple, impressing the men who impressed the nation. He asked the wisest questions and then provided the best answers. There were no signs of abuse, hunger, fear or discomfort. Before He was even a teenager, Jesus seemed to be in His element, doing what He was born to do.

This event appeared to be an opportunity for Mary and Joseph to stand back, enjoy the moment, and say: "This is our son, our boy, the Messiah, sent by God for you Israel." They could have watched and rejoiced in their son's fulfillment of destiny. But they did none of that. There were tears, but not of joy. When His parents saw Him, they were astonished, stricken by panic. Jesus' parents were disappointed and afraid. Then the three days of anxiety found release in this one statement:

> "Son, why have you treated us like this? Your father and
> I have been anxiously searching for you." [2]

Mary and Joseph took it personally and felt rejected. They were relieved that they had finally found Him, but understandably angered because of the anguish experienced during the search. Then Jesus asked back, "Why were you searching for me? Didn't you know I had to be in my Father's house?" [3]

Depending on the tone you used when questioning your own parents, the reply of Jesus may sound arrogant, immature, or just plain rebellious. Yet, we know as a scriptural fact, that nothing impure was coming out of His heart. Therefore, His argument may be interpreted like this:

> "Explain something to me mom. Did an angel not come to you before you were even pregnant and told you who I was? Remember the whole government-on-His-shoulders, Savior-to-the-world deal? Was it not you Dad, who had a dream, and were led by God to care for me, to protect me in Egypt? Do you guys not remember the meaning of my first name? Do you not know what I came to do? Because I do, and now, more than ever. I am meant to be here! This is my calling! And you, of all people, should understand."

There He was, a perfect son, on His first attempt to be His own man. Rightly following His heart to do the Father's will. Yet the answer given by his earthly parents in this moment of discovery is a resounding, "No."

Jesus had a revelation of His high calling, but those who were expected to lift Him, as all moms and dads should, instead, shut Him down. Maybe Mary and Joseph could not see the full picture here, but out of everyone alive, they had more revelation of Jesus the Christ. They understood that they could not keep their son forever. They heard from God that He was alive for a wonderful purpose. However, their parental instinct did not allow them to fully understand. Either anxiety fogged twelve years of supernatural insight or they chose to ignore it because of the price they knew it demanded.

Someone had to decide the course of action and there were only two choices in this scenario. Choice number one was for Jesus to start

His earthly ministry right there. He had the attention of the top minds of the nation and He captured their imagination with His wisdom and understanding. He could have been known as the young prophet who lives a perfect life according to the Law of Moses. He could have said, "Actually Mary and Joseph I created you and I'm your superior so you should submit." And he would have had a good point!

Choice number two was less exciting: submission to His parents. Which is exactly what He did, for Jesus "went down to Nazareth *with* them and was obedient *to* them." [4]

No human likes to hear the word no, especially when you are so sure of the yes. This story shows us one of the most crucial decisions Jesus ever made as a man. It gives us insight into the character of Jesus, His spiritual maturity and His willingness to yield.

You see, proper leadership requires submission to the authorities that are before us. Jesus therefore made His own mission come under submission to the task that God had given Mary and Joseph. He honored their calling as parents before He honored His calling as the Teacher. He chose integrity over influence, purity over ministry, and humility over pride. And because of that decision, history had to wait eighteen years, for the young Jesus to become the 30-year-old Christ, and fully manifest His destiny.

Hundreds of uninspired books have been written to explain what happened during those eighteen years of the life of Jesus. There are false stories about His travels and studies. Different religions put Him in direct contact with their leaders, and there are unsupported reports of Him being influenced by other teachings and messiahs.

Meanwhile, the Bible finds no need to fill the eighteen-year gap with anything other than the submission of Christ as a son. While

Mary treasured in her heart all the things that happened back in Jerusalem, Jesus went back to Nazareth, was obedient to His parents, and grew in wisdom, stature, and in favor with God and with men. [5] God the Son looked into His earthly mother's eyes and chose to love her before Himself. He searched His heart and made the right choice to obey the request of His adopted father Joseph. He was tempted with power, arrogance and pride but even when it was His heavenly right to step into what He was sent to do; the boy, the man, the son, obeyed.

Jesus took the highest road, even when there was a legitimate alternative available. The Son of God found it to be the best use of his time on earth during that season to just be a son to his mom and dad. Obedience was the best investment into His maturity.

This story is now a challenge to all the generations who believe with all of their heart, "We got it!" His choice to be a son first is an open invitation to everyone who has ever been denied the right to step into their calling, at this present moment. We have all suffered some legitimate loss of destiny at the hands of our fathers. We have all felt stuck and blamed it on our parents. However, Jesus' choice suggests a different perspective.

What if we have not grown because we chose not to stick by them? What if home was the perfect set-up for increase and favor? What if going back to your Nazareth is the best investment into your growth, your stature, your favor?

Pastors, leaders, moms and dads, who in our eyes became thieves of dreams and vision, in the eyes of heaven, provided us with an opportunity. Even when you know without a shadow of a doubt that you are in the right place, if they ask, go back to Nazareth and be submissive to them. It is there that the wrong place for right now, becomes the best place to grow in God. Jesus chose sonship. When was the last time you did?

Time to Shine!

Fast-forward eighteen years to the time Jesus was 30 and attending a wedding in Cana of Galilee. Jesus' mother and His disciples had also been invited to the ceremony. Abruptly, at some point during the party, the same mom who had previously asked Jesus to come back with them to Nazareth, the lady who had requested the Son of God to stop being awesome until the time had come, approached Jesus and said:

> "'They have no more wine.'
> And Jesus replied to her, 'Woman, why do you involve me? My hour has not yet come.'" [6]

The Son of God had been waiting for the anointed moment to unveil His identity as the miracle maker. The timing was not right; not this day; not at this wedding; not in John chapter 2. Yet, His mother orders the servants: "Do whatever he tells you."

Six stone jars stood nearby each capable of holding about thirty gallons of water. Without saying anything else to Mary, Jesus asked the servants to "fill the jars with water." And they filled them to the brim. Then, He told them to "draw some out and take it to the master of the banquet."

The master of the banquet tasted the water and realized it had been turned into wine. He did not comprehend where the wine had come from and he was puzzled. "Everyone brings out the choice wine first and then the inexpensive after the guests have had too much to drink; but you have saved the best till now," he said to the bridegroom. It was Jesus' first miracle.

It is not clear if Mary knew specifically what Jesus was going to do at the wedding, but she released Him to be the one who solved the problem. She knew His identity as Savior and here was a wedding that needed saving. Even if the timing, according to the divine plan, was off target, it was so right for Jesus to begin His ministry after His mother released Him from hers.

Jesus lived as a son under the authority of the woman He knew as *mom*. He revealed His glory, not at the appointed occasion, but when Mary, the one who breastfed Him as a baby, asked for it to become the right time. Mary did not possess more power or more revelation than Jesus; neither was she a controlling mother who manipulated her son. She allowed Him to wait eighteen years, but she understood that the world could wait no longer. The King of Glory turned water into wine, His first miraculous sign, because there was a woman pregnant with hope for Israel.

There is a Biblical appeal for sons and daughters to get their parents' blessing. It is a fundamental principle found in Scripture and established in multiple stories in the Old and New Testament. We may think there is no way we can find anything Godly back where we came from, but, what if our prophetic destiny is found in our parents' home? What if the main people we need to start manifesting sonship to, are in fact our own father and mother?

There was no fear in the heart of Jesus about "missing" God's timing. He understood delegated authority so He trusted His eternal Father even while living under the guidance of His temporary parents. Then His three years of being everything that they raised him up to be, finally came. Now it was here, when the son of the carpenter, the son of Mary, was fully released to reveal Himself, as the Son of God. Jesus had every argument to discredit the fatherhood of Joseph, but He knew the holy ways of His heavenly Father: *"Honor your father and your mother, that your days may be long in the land that the Lord your God is giving you."* [7]

He chose to honor the man who was the head of His household, followed him from Egypt to Nazareth, learned his trade and carried His family's identity even throughout His full-time ministry. [8]

Even at the cross, Jesus took care of family business. He allowed Mary to come under the guardianship of his trusted friend John. While he took the sin of the entire world on His shoulders, while He endured the most epic battle in all of history, Jesus made sure, that mom would be ok.

Sonship to our family should never stop in the face of great ministry. Even when Jesus had to walk a different road than the one his immediate family would have Him walk, He visited, He honored, He remained a son. They were not always in agreement but at the end of His earthly ministry, His mother and his brothers became part of the movement of those who would believe in Him, and change the world. [9]

What does it mean to honor your parents?
Kids: Obey your parents. Adolescents: Respect your parents.
Adults: Care for your aging parents.

— MARK DRISCOLL

Know Where You Come From

I don't blame you if you skip genealogies in the Bible—I've done it myself multiple times. You try to move forward with your daily reading, but feel convicted that you skipped actual-printed-Holy-Scripture. So, you go back to the long list of old Hebrew names and with a serious face, skim through them quickly. It feels better.

There are genealogies for the descendants of 23 people in the Old and New Testament. The writers, inspired by the Holy Spirit, found incredible value in showing the family trees of these individuals, of which Jesus was one. In fact, He got two different lists. His list in the book of Matthew goes from Abraham to Jesus. Luke's list, on the other hand, goes from Jesus back to Adam. Each evangelist tried to communicate a different message through the same background.

Matthew's Gospel focuses on the redemptive history, from Abraham to Jesus, and also on His royalty by highlighting King David in the timeline. This genealogy screams to the first-century reader, "This is the King" and "Here comes the Kingdom."

On the other hand, Luke's genealogy goes back to Adam with a focus on the humanity of Jesus. It shows Christ as one of us, a son of the first man. It is a reminder that, through Adam sin entered the world, but through Jesus it was defeated.

In the same manner, there is a story of redemption in every one of our genealogies. The fact that you are reading this book and chasing after the things of the Spirit proves that God is getting "the final word" in your DNA. Similarly to you, Jesus had a Granny Tamar who slept with her father-in-law, Rahab the lying prostitute, mama Ruth, the result of incest, and Bathsheba who committed adultery with King David (the great grandfather who seduced a naked lady and murdered a righteous man). And it is from this lineage we get the Son of God, perfect in all His ways.

This is proof that there is no background story in your bloodline that can outwork the power of the Father in your present. Your last name celebrates God's work of redemption; it is not a reminder of a filthy past. If you were brought up by Godly parents who loved you, cared for you and showed you His ways, it is because of His work of redemption. If you were brought up by abusive, alcoholic or absent parents, your life is just as much a story of redemption.

Every genealogy in Scripture gives us a picture of the historical baggage men and women of God brought to the day of their transformation and the fulfillment of their purpose. If the Bible informed us only of the good people and their super amazing achievements, then we would never get to comprehend the mighty grace of God that is "showing love to a thousand generations of those who love me and keep my commandments." [10]

The past will not determine your present. If you see it through the eyes of the Father, it can actually empower your future.

The Key to Redeeming

Although, the love of God is unconditional, there is at least one condition to receive it. He loves us still, no matter what, but we can hinder the access to that love with our choices. Fortunately, Jesus showed us a way to get rid of most of the issues that separate us from the Father's healing flow.

The solution is called forgiveness. It is the key that empowers us to be free, and the tool that enables us to free others. It is the gift that can change the look of our lineage and the expectation for our inheritance. But, it is also a nonnegotiable clause in this Kingdom of grace.

"For if you forgive men when they sin against you, your heavenly Father will also forgive you. But if you do not forgive men their sins, your Father will not forgive your sins." [11]

Though some types of wounds can make the lack of forgiveness seem justifiable, God's condition for forgiveness cannot be skipped. Yes, *you* have been sinned against in the most horrific way—and usually by the people who were meant to show you the most incredible love. Yes, there are fathers and mothers in your history who have wounded you beyond recognition. It will feel like they don't deserve to be forgiven, but you cannot afford *not* to forgive them.

Whilst I ministered in Sheffield, my wife's hometown in England, a woman laughed uncontrollably through one of my teachings. At the end of the meeting, she approached me, and told me a vision she kept seeing like a clip on repeat. She could see her father, who had sexually abused her as a child, being carried on the shoulders of Jesus on His way to Calvary.

For the first time in her life, the woman discovered the joy of forgiveness. Every time she saw the image, like a wave crashing against her soul, she went deeper in honesty as she repeated in a whisper "I forgive you dad" That evening she realized, that Jesus carried her sin, but also the sin committed against her. She then accepted the truth, that Jesus became one with her as a victim but also one with her dad as the predator. As Jesus hanged naked at the cross, beaten all over his face, his back and his genitals, this 33-year-old virgin who had kept himself pure, experienced sexual abuse. At the very same time, while He endured the horror of being publicly exposed, He took upon Himself every sexual sin committed in secret.

This revelation was no longer something this lady heard as a story or understood as theology. That day, led by the Holy Spirit, she was able to fully let go of the demand of justice in her heart. She became a manifestation of the grace of Jesus towards her own dad. She left the room in a mix of tears and laughter and as a daughter who walked in radical freedom, the kind of freedom that Jesus has for us all.

Our parents' sin against us makes us weak, fearful and angry, and we cannot be blamed for that. But the hard floor of bitterness and the bars of regret, that give shape to the prison of judgment, will never be an enjoyable home.

Think of forgiveness as skydiving. As we travel 124 mph towards the ground, we have no option but to open our parachute. We always have a choice, but we don't *really* have a choice. We have the "right" to stay offended with our parents, but that "right" might lead us to become worse than them. Instead, when we release them from our judgment it will produce Godliness. To gain what we have lost, we must first let go; we have got to trust the Father even when we do not agree. It will be impossible for us to truly manifest sonship to God and to men, unless we forgive.

Whilst I was writing this chapter, one of the students at our School of Revival shared with the class a testimony of forgiveness. She told us of the many times she had gone through the motions of forgiveness, but as Adam Walton, our School director, shared on connecting to the specific pain our parents have inflicted, she began to forgive from the heart. It was later on that very same day when her mother called. She wanted to initiate relationship again, and they shared their love with each other which they had not done for a long time.

This is a spiritual dynamic that is initiated when we release our parents from our judgments and send a message in the spirit that we want to be their children. It might take a bit of time to regain trust, but forgive we must!

Therefore, God invites us to get in touch with the deep pain the fathers and mothers in our lives have caused us; to look into the eyes of Jesus and ask Him to teach us how to forgive. And, as the Holy Spirit empowers us to walk in mercy towards others, remember that we have been saved because God walks in mercy towards us. It may not be easy, but it will be freeing, and above all, it will be worth it.

You are now invited to open up the parachute and enjoy the view from God's perspective, in the realm of His goodness and grace.

> *To forgive is to set a prisoner free and discover*
> *that the prisoner was you.* — LEWIS B SMEEDS

If you want the freedom that comes through forgiveness, I invite you to consciously read and complete the following declaration:

> Thank you Jesus for dying in my place that I might be forgiven. By an act of my will I now choose to forgive those who have hurt me or sinned against me. I forgive _____ for (be specific). I give the gift of unconditional forgiveness to each one of these. They owe

me nothing. I entrust them to you God. I bless each of them in your name.

Lord, I ask you to forgive me for my ungodly response to offense and pain. I have judged with wrong attitudes and words, in bitterness and anger. I ask you now to forgive me for my ungodly and sinful responses.

Forgive me for these, and any other sinful, hidden judgments in my heart with which I have given the enemy legal rights to torment me. I choose to repent of these ungodly and sinful responses and practices. Thank you Jesus that I am forgiven, and thank you for setting me free. I am a child of *Abba* and I will walk in forgiveness towards all. In your name, Amen.

SONSHIP TO YOUR OWN

*"He chose integrity over influence, purity over ministry
and humility over pride."*

Jesus chose sonship first, it was his first priority. He spent 30 years of his life submitting to his parents.

What is the state of your heart toward your earthly parents?
Our parents are not perfect and we don't make excuses for that, but there is a blessing that comes from honouring our parents for the good we see in them.

Do you have a heart of sonship towards your own parents?
Do you need to restore relationship with them in any way? It is possible to honour and bless them, and have hearts of sons and daughters towards our parents while acknowledging their own weakness.

Have you in any way disowned your family heritage?
Or can you see where God has been in it, blessing the generations? Ask the Holy Spirit to show you how He has been moving in your family line and what He sees.

Forgiveness is key to walking in sonship. When we are able to forgive our parents we unlock our hearts to walk in sonship towards them. Unforgiveness is not an option if you want to fully manifest sonship to God and to men.

Use the prayer Carlos outlines to forgive those you know you are holding unforgiveness towards.

CHAPTER TEN

THE PURSUIT

To a young leader: Don't try to be Batman in your Robin season.

— TOMMY TENNEY

Some of us social-media users like to impress our friends with quotes that communicate whatever idea is soaking in our heart, but with someone else's superior choice of words. As Dorothy L. Sayers said, "I always have a quotation for everything for it saves original thinking."

I read a quote a couple of years ago and without hesitation, I copied and pasted it onto my Facebook wall, "A person without a mentor is like a sailboat without a breeze." Comments were quickly added to my page, but to my surprise, most of them were in disagreement. I read them, disappointed as I realized that we are living in a generation that is willing to participate in plastic relationships formed and developed on the internet, but unwilling to become dependent on actual human beings who can help, equip and support. For too long arts and media have been idolizing rebellion and demonizing respect, and it has taken a toll on us.

As I read the word *mentor*, it sounded almost equivalent to *father*. Maybe, I was finally getting comfortable with the idea of having older and more experienced people speak into my life. I was getting cozy with the fact that their encouragement and direction could be necessary for when important decisions were needed. Perhaps I would even be okay with a certain degree of dependency on such mentors. In fact it has become breeze to my sails.

The problem with the conflicting mentalities I faced in each comment is that if the majority of us struggle with the understanding of fatherhood, then the next generation is destined to pay the price. When our turn to be the mentors comes, we will find ourselves with no sons to guide and no daughters to empower. This fatherless outlook towards life must be broken, "For the creation waits with eager longing for the revealing of the sons of God." [1]

The Son's Quest

We all expect the fathers in our lives to be the ones who pursue us, the children. Most of us crave a father who takes the time to call. Everyone likes the boss who cares about his employees, and I know most people prefer the pastor who follows up on relationships. Our natural demand for attention is a normal longing that needs no correction, but we also need to understand that the dynamics in the Kingdom of God are usually the other way around. It is *our* responsibility—as sons—to pursue the fathers, and it is in that pursuit that we find our inheritance. In the first book of Kings, the story of Elijah and Elisha has a handle on this principle. The relationship of the two prophets started when God ordered Elijah to "anoint Elisha, son of Shaphat, to succeed him." The old prophet found the young prophet as he plowed with twelve yoke of oxen. He went up to him and threw his cloak around his shoulders, which provoked Elisha to leave his oxen and run after Elijah. "Let me kiss my father and mother goodbye," Elisha said, "and then I will come with you." The fierce prophet replied, "Go back! What have I done to you?"

Poor Elisha! It is day one of following the man of God as a spiritual son, and already miscommunication.

Elisha left him momentarily; went back home, and slaughtered his oxen. He then burned the plowing equipment, cooked the meat, and gave it to the people to eat. This decision was a statement to his heart, to his community and to his God. It proclaimed that everything that had been his livelihood was now the testimony of his surrender. When he killed his cattle he placed all his trust in God to provide. When he burned the equipment, he got rid of any resource to come back to. And, when he fed the people with his sacrifice, he gave them permission to keep him accountable to the promise he had made.

Then, after sharing this farewell meal with his father, mother, and friends, the newly chosen prophet "went after Elijah, and ministered unto him."

God decided to call and anoint Elisha through the relationship he now had with Elijah. All the young prophet could do was to accept and receive what was given to him. He had no power to make it happen, but he was brave enough to jump right into the unknown. This invitation was from heaven but the pursuit was Elisha's choice.

However, just as we heard nothing from Jesus' eighteen years of sonship, from 1 Kings 19:20 until 2 Kings 3:11 we read nothing of Elisha's. What we do have are the incredible words the great prophet Elijah shared with the people of God. We read about the miracles, signs and wonders done through his ministry, but only one thing is said of his assistant.

He was known by others as the man who would "pour water on the hands of Elijah," but this position as a servant enabled him to observe the prophet's life first hand. That intimacy so affected Elisha that he grew a desire for what Elijah had. All he gleaned from the prophet during his time of servanthood did not diminish his desire to get a double portion of the spirit of the man he now saw as a mentor. Eventually, the day arrived for Elijah the prophet to depart. The Bible narrates two occasions in which another company of prophets meet with Elisha. These men of God, with the gift of spiritual insight, ask Elisha, "Don't you know what the Lord is up to? He's going to take your master away from you today."

The prophets knew Elijah was going to be taken, but their insight about Elisha's identity was limited to his duties as a servant. Elijah was a master indeed, but the revelation Elisha manifested and the way he walked with Elijah was more characteristic of a son.

In this the last day of their journey together, Elijah and Elisha are still mis-communicating. The prophet asked him to leave three times, but the disciple chose to stay. Even when the company of prophets challenged his prophetic gift, he chose to humble himself and wait. Elisha knew what was about to happen, but he had no control over the destiny of his spiritual father; all he could do was to stick around and wait for the glorious leftovers.

When the moment arrived for Elijah, the prophet, to be taken up, He asked the man who was always beside him, "What can I do for you?" So Elisha requested a double portion of his spirit. I know that it would sound "theologically correct" if Elisha had asked for a double portion of God's Spirit, but that's not what he said. He asked for a double portion of Elijah's spirit; his father's intangible dna.

The condition for Elisha to receive this spirit, was to stick around a while longer, and stay close till the expected departure. And as they were walking and talking together, chariots and horses of fire appeared and took Elijah on a whirlwind up to heaven. When Elisha saw this, he cried out: *"My father! My father!* The chariots and horsemen of Israel!" And Elisha saw him no more.

On the words, *"My father! My father!"* rested the revelation that the sons of the prophets could not grasp. This is how Elisha saw Elijah, and this is why he served him well. You see, Elisha was not as interested in his own gifting, he had a desire for his father's mantle. He was not in the pursuit of an increase of *his* calling, but for his father's legacy to continue through him. Elisha saw himself as a son and that made him stick around till the end.

After Elijah was taken, the young prophet "took hold of his own garment and tore it in two." Elisha undressed himself and took upon the mantle of the man who had become his father. After that, he struck the water, it divided in half, and he crossed over; an identical miracle to Elijah's last sign. Thus, the company of the prophets from Jericho concluded, "The spirit of Elijah is resting on Elisha." [2]

Elisha duplicated the man that had gone before him and did not interpret doing so as a threat to his own calling. Moreover, it enabled him to do twice the miracles that his mentor did. God endowed Elijah to empower his successor. And Elisha, either by divine revelation or cultural wisdom, understood the principle of pursuing the father-son-ministry relation.

I hope you're getting the picture by now. We all need a father, and like Elisha we all have a father figure available in our life. God will always pave the road for his sons to become fathers to others through His ministry. What we need to understand is our necessity to pursue those fathers who God has already commissioned for us. What we now need is a double portion of the spirit of *Elisha*.

Our Opportunity

When parents pursue the children it can be seen as manipulation, but when the children pursue their parents, it is always an invitation. In the story of the prodigal son I shared in chapter one, it is evident that no matter how much the father cared for his younger boy or how incredibly loving he was on his return, the father never went to the foreign lands for his rescue; he waited at home. The Father that Jesus came to reveal is an eternally loving Father, merciful in all His ways, but He expects us to be the ones who come. Pursuing fathers is an eternal principle to be discovered today.

Yet we find ourselves constantly trying to find faults in leaders and mothers and pastors, finding justifications and reasons why not to follow. Most of the time the faults are legitimate and the reasons are valid, but the mantle is not for those who win arguments, it is for those who are able to humble themselves and think the best. Most of us will walk with no mantle tomorrow, because we have not pursued the shoulders that carry them today. We are constantly aware of the things that need to change in our churches for a better future, but we need to earn the right to be heard by those that God has entrusted to lead the saints in the present state.

Our spiritual father, whether it is a pastor, an older friend, a cell group leader, or our own biological father, is not even close to being perfect. Their available time might be limited by their busy schedules. They might also carry past wounds and have walls around their hearts. Maybe they never had a true mentor themselves to lead and guide them through life.

But now, more than ever, we have to allow our hearts to hear their direction, to receive their feedback and to learn from their correction. We need to have confidence in God's ability to lead us through our dad and moms. We might not agree with everything they say, but our hearts should be open to be shaped and challenged even in debates.

Saying, "Yes" to spiritual fathers is a statement of trust towards your heavenly Father. He knew the time and place where you would be born and the people around you are part of His plan for your greatness. My wife and I made a decision not to get offended when the opportunities arise. We rather learn, continually pursue and believe the best of those that lead us. During our personal walk together as a family, most of the supernatural fruit we have experienced has come from a direct root to these spiritual fathers. And all of us have a divine calling to embrace the concepts of sonship by pursuit, surrender and emulation. The popular proverb says, "If you are the smartest person in the room, you are in the wrong room." Start finding those that have gone before you and take the invitation from heaven to get into their rooms.

Stop expecting them to control you and start trusting God to lead you with them. It is the culture of heaven, manifested on earth and revealed through His Word.

Choose the Right Shoulders

Sir Isaac Newton once said, "If I have seen a little further it is by standing on the shoulders of giants." Now I wonder, what if we have similar shoulders available to us? And if they are, why is it that only a few get to unleash their full life potential like Newton did?

We all have gigantic shoulders in Father God. He is a dad willing to lift us higher, show us His ways and bless us beyond our wildest dreams. However, the life of a son is not just about accepting God as our father, it is about the acceptance of our earthly fathers and our capacity to set them free from our judgments.

We have giants all around us; people available to lend their shoulders and show us the road ahead. There are men and women, ready and able to support and disciple us into the fullness of our calling in Christ Jesus.

Most of the time the things that we call "new" in God, are really old wells that were not transferred from one generation to another. These wells have been lost in the desert of past movements and the present generation goes thirsty without the map to find them. Yet, I have heard a hopeful message from my in-laws, my own parents and most of my spiritual leaders. They are giving us an invitation to use their experience as our launching pad. They are longing to deploy what they have received already, so that their ceiling becomes our floor. These fathers and mothers are out there, drawing from old wells and we just need to find them and draw with them. At that point, we shall release the things that are legitimately new while standing alongside the oasis we have enjoyed with the older generation.

All of us are full of prophetic promise, but some have not been able to open their heart to the possibility of sharing their purpose with a father. For some, past experiences have fogged their lenses, and the image of a father awakens disappointment. Others have not been looking or might have assumed that we were created to make it on our own, to draw out our own path, to create our own destiny.

If you have been around the Father's presence for more than ten minutes you know that He is a God of purpose and destiny. We know through Scripture that He loves to call, empower and send out. His idea of a healthy relationship is to share mission, and God the Father is in the business of sharing. He is passionate about giving you a vision for your life, because a person without a vision is a person without a future, and a person without a future will always return to his past.

Growth is easily achieved when we as trees are planted in good soil and close to the river. The problem comes when we try to grow in the dry land of independence, away from the many waters. There, our trunks will struggle to grow strong and when we do bear fruit, it will be bitter and unhealthy.

Too many of my friends, as anointed and willing as they are, cannot see further ahead. "Stuck" seems to be the word that best explains their current vision. They strive to know where they should go or even what they want to do. And when they do discover it, the rocky journey of the one-man-show steals away their hope. This is why

God gave us fathers and mothers: to show us the way, and to train us in His ways. With them we are able to find a better road than the one we are struggling with today. God's invitation for us is to open our hearts to the men and women of authority around us, so that we can be lifted up from our current viewpoint, to see what is available beyond our orphan perspective.

The first thing we need to do is recognize that we need them. The second, is to look at those shoulders as a God given gift from heaven; an upgrade to our past; a hope for our future.

We are all God's creation, but to be sons, we have to make a choice. Let's get on those giants' shoulders so that we can become giants ourselves.

Let's Get Practical

Tell me that pursuing a father is hard, and I will agree with you. You might have tried in the past but they were busy. Maybe you were self-conscious and did not want to be a burden; or thought that they had enough on their plates already. Sometimes, when we want to approach them, they seem uninterested. Other times, their answers to our questions were precisely what we did *not* want to hear; and other times their counsel has not helped us in the time of need. Pursue them still, and make yourself unavoidable! My recommendations are not to be taken as an encouragement for a new breed of stalkers. That's the last thing any leader needs. Besides, it is hard for fathers to trust anyone who obviously comes to them for what *they* can get out of the deal. Our eyes must not be set upon our personal gain, but on ways to bless *them*.

What spiritual fathers and mothers need are sons and daughters who are ready to carry their legacy. They are looking for people who are willing to honor what they have accomplished in their lifetime. The desire is for descendants who are eager to take the inheritance to the next level and through the next generation.

When I go to my fathers, I know that they are prepared to bless me, fund my vision and help me carry the load, but I still approach them as a son that wants to do the same for them. I try to pay the bill when I invite them out for a meal. I try to be present to serve and ask questions. I am intentional in my pursuit of a relationship.

I also try to find common ground between my fathers and me. I speak honor and friendship, not a self-serving message. I take no offense in the fact that I have to organize our times together. I don't see it as a sin when those times are postponed because of their other priorities. I am set on making that connection, and will not allow my heart to be contaminated with the disappointment of unmet expectations. If this principle is true, and in the kingdom it's the sons who pursue the fathers, then I pursue.

All these efforts may seem too ideal, too perfect or too radical; and in a way they are. The only father that can lead, mentor and guide us in perfect love at all times, is God the Father. And even with Him we might get disappointed when His ways are higher than ours.

Jesus is by far the greatest senior leader the world has ever seen and when talking about relationships, he said to "Do to others as you would have them do to you." [3] His encouragement is to learn to honor the people that lead us, even when they don't lead us as we would lead others.

The Son of God led his men with valor and wisdom. He gave them opportunities to fail, to learn and to shine. Jesus spoke words of life, comfort and direction to his followers. Yet, while being "The Way, the Truth and the Life," His main role was to lead them all to God His Father.

Intentionally or involuntarily, your earthly and spiritual fathers will lead you to the perfect Father. You might not recognize it, but even when they fail, they create the perfect scenario for you to run into your Heavenly Daddy's arms. When they reject you, He will receive you. When they fail at meeting you, He will open up His schedule. When they miscommunicate with you, He will share His heart of love for you *and* His heart of love for them.

If we can agree to honor our fathers and mothers then we are sowing seeds that will empower our own spiritual sons and daughters to maturity. If you don't go after your fathers they probably will not come after you; and that is a barrier in your heart that needs to be broken. Be prepared to pay the price of sonship, because it is worth it, and your destiny demands it.

Fathers will Understand

The greatest feeling I have experienced as a father, is to have my sons, Alejandro and Sebastián, pursue my company. I have changed Alejandro's diaper, fed him rice and beans and attended to his needs since he was born in 2011. I have surrendered my life to serving him for two and a half years, but now, I get the best reward. My first-born calls out "papi" and invites me to come into his room. While in the room, He points at me and says, "No phone, no phone." He demands my full attention, which means, my precious iPhone is not allowed in his play area. Then he closes the door behind him and says, "Bye, bye mami" (mom); "bye, bye hermano" (brother). He finds a specific book or toy that has connected us in the past, and, with a big smile on his face and a twinkle in his eye, says, "Papi y me" which in perfect *Spanglish* means, "Daddy and me."

I cannot escape this glorious prison of joy that my boy prepares for me. Nothing ever tasted sweeter than those daddy and son moments with Alejandro. And now, I get a double dose, when my youngest, Sebastián, pushes through the closed door to join the connection.

The greatest gift my sons give me is their desire to be themselves around their daddy. They know I can teach them so they get hungry to learn. They know that I can play with them, so they initiate the wrestle. They know that I will correct them; yet still they approach me with confidence.

We all need to be parented in trust, and in the depths of our hearts, we truly want that connection. We might feel too old to acknowledge the need, but the need remains the same. Sons who pursue will get fathers who respond.

I began to ask these questions while teaching on this topic of spiritual sonship, "Who in this room was taught by their parents on how to deal with budget and personal finances?" Usually, in a crowd smaller than ten, only two hands go up.

"Who here had a proper sex-talk with their mom and dad?" In a crowd of more than fifty people, usually 10% raise their hands.

"Who here decided to learn one of their parents' trade and is now walking in a greater level of knowledge or success than them?" In a crowd of any size, usually only a couple of hands go up.

The wrong value on independence, both in parents and their children, have robbed our different age groups from the opportunity to learn and grow together. Yet, as sons and daughters we now can reverse this trend; let it be on us! Let us build relationship with spiritual parents. Let us make the phone calls to those who have already walked the road. Let it be on us to ask the questions and to shadow for the mantle. And if it takes the rest of our lives, then they will be days well spent.

Are you willing to look past the imperfections of others and find your Elijah? They might not be walking as you wish them to walk, but it might be because we have not been honoring them the way they deserve. Come on sons and daughters, pursue the best out of your fathers!

Personally, I wish I had done it more with my dad, my grandfather and my first pastor. My hope is that you understand this godly principle, put it into practice, and end up with no regrets; just victories, growth and inherited favor.

Big shoulders are around you, I suggest you start climbing.

STUDY GUIDE: CHAPTER 10
THE PURSUIT

*"The first thing we need to do is recognize
that we need spiritual fathers."*

Pursuit

Through the story of Elijah and Elisha, Carlos highlights the importance of pursuing spiritual fathers. **What do you think about this concept? Do you have any reservations? If so, can you identify where these are coming from?**

Can you identify a spiritual father in your life that you could pursue?

Admonition

Are you willing to receive direction and feedback from them, even correction?

Are you willing to look past the imperfections of others and find your Elijah?

> *"Our eyes must not be set on personal gain but*
> *on ways to bless them."*

CHAPTER ELEVEN

ORIGINAL IMITATION

Tell me and I forget,
teach me and I may remember,
involve me and I will learn.

— BENJAMIN FRANKLIN

Our current Western-Christianity model is jam packed with countless guides and multiple instructors. There are thousands of good men and women in ministry with the ability to promote their teachings, share their revelations and sell their latest product. I get to join the pack by leading a church in North Carolina and by writing the book you have in your hands. We are all instructors for the body of Christ and we carry a message with the potential to change people's perspectives about certain ideas.

Don't get me wrong; I love my countless instructors! Pastor Morris from Gateway church in Dallas TX has instructed me with incredible concepts of leadership for a growing local church. Bill Johnson from Bethel, Redding, has given me at least one powerhouse quote for every sermon I have preached in the last five years. In a book written for ladies, Joyce Meyer helped me to manage my emotions in a Godly way. Even the journey I am taking you on began when I read Gene Edward's beautiful book, *A Tale of Three Kings.*

The truth is though that I barely know one of them personally. I can call them teachers but it would be naive to call them fathers. Billy Graham preached the sermon that got me saved. Steve Hill led the meetings in Brownsville which made me fall in love with revival. Yiye Avila lived a life of prayer, humility and integrity that inspires me to this day and, just like them, there are many more instructors to choose from. Leaders who are wise, experienced and able to communicate their message to a bigger audience. You can download their podcast, you can read their blog and attend one of their conferences, but you could never do life with them.

So here is the warning/invitation/instruction from the apostle Paul, "I do not write these things to make you ashamed, but to admonish you as my beloved children. For though you have *countless guides* in Christ, you *do not have many fathers.* For I became your father in Christ Jesus through the gospel. *I urge you, then, be imitators of me.*" [1]

The great Apostle paints a simple equation for long lasting results: Imitate a father, become one yourself. It was the formula used by the early church leaders so that the advancement of the Kingdom would not depend on just one or two individuals. As we saw in the previous chapter, our responsibility is to pursue a father, and that pursuit has purpose. It is leading towards greatness, and to your own fatherhood. The New Testament includes letters specifically written by spiritual fathers to their spiritual sons, two of which are from Paul to Timothy. The bond between these two characters resembles the kind of father-son relationship that has the potential to transform the world. The way Timothy related to Paul gave him not only the opportunity to be a son to the apostle, but also to become a great father himself.

Timothy's life was transformed during one of Paul's first ministry trips. The young man quickly left his family and became involved in the evangelistic work of the ex-terrorist. There was something about Timothy that made Paul write "I have no one like him,"[2] and affirm later, "you know his proven character, that as a son with his father he served with me in the gospel."

These men shared the glory and the burden of church leadership. Timothy's name appears as co-author of 2 Corinthians, Philippians, Colossians, 1 Thessalonians, 2 Thessalonians, and Philemon. There is no doubt that Paul as a father believed in Tim's gift, calling and destiny. He was involved with his family and was constantly encouraging him. He became Timothy's mentor in life but also his number one fan.

In response, Timothy provided care and assistance even while his mentor was in prison. He continued the mission they had started together and carried the flame of Paul's genuine faith and message. It is estimated that the church in Ephesus that Paul left Timothy in charge of, had at least 100,000 members. Historians agree that Timothy would have been in his late twenties or mid thirties when he was appointed as overseer. Paul handed down one of the fastest growing and most successful churches of all times to his young spiritual son.

Fathering is God's design to grow a healthy generation in the essentials of His Kingdom. It is Heaven's offer for us to return to His original model. I will keep on learning from my instructors and I encourage you to do the same. Allow those who are gifted in worship and music to lead you in love songs to Jesus. Follow the different outpourings of God around the world. Honor the diversity of revelation that the body of Christ manifests during the particular lifespan you live in. But, whatever you do, pay attention to Paul's advice; do not miss your chance to find a father to imitate.

There are giants of the faith, with no platform to fame, that come to instruct our churches every Sunday. We can find many local church leaders, with the wisdom of Solomon, who have chosen to surrender their lives for small towns and intimate crowds. There are soccer moms, high school teachers and small business owners who are willing to invest time and energy to make you a real success. It is time to open your eyes to the parents around you and become a "beloved and faithful son in the Lord" to one of them.

Don't Fear Imitation

Right after I made my decision to serve Pastor Tito as long as God would want me to, Duncan Smith visited our church for a weekend of Holy Spirit fun. This was his second visit to the local church in Puerto Rico, but this time, he travelled by himself. We had three amazing days of teaching and ministry with many wonders and physical healings.

On his last evening with us, we had a meal overlooking the ocean while savoring fresh snapper cooked Caribbean style (don't worry, I'm sure you will experience it in Heaven). Back in our apartment while we shared stories from the weekend, Duncan began to ask me questions about my dreams and my plans for the future. He was caring, pastoral, eager to challenge and even to correct me. I was in tears again, as I went through a heart healing session with one of my best friends and my wife tag-team ministering.

The next day Duncan woke up to the sound of our neighbors' rooster, and soon after we began our journey to the airport for his flight back to Toronto. When I returned home a couple of hours later, Catherine was still asleep. So rather than waking her up, I ended up taking some time to process what had happened the night before.

I found myself surrounded by God's kindness all over again. It was inevitable, I fell on my knees and began to weep. But surprisingly, an unintended prayer began to mix in with the worship I was expressing, "Jesus, I want to imitate Duncan, as He imitates you."

It sounded weird coming out of my mouth. I was very comfortable with the idea of imitating Jesus, but imitating another human being? Never! I mean, I liked Duncan and respected his leadership and abilities but I was my own man. God had a plan for my life. I was able to make it happen on my own. Me and Jesus were enough, right?

Yet on that day it felt good and right as my spirit spoke it, "I want to imitate Duncan." I had overlooked the verses of Paul asking for others to imitate him in the past and I had never expected those words to be used by me.

I remember nothing else after that prayer. Catherine got up, we went to work that Monday and continued to happily serve our church family in Camuy.

Duncan called me a couple of months later as I was having dinner with my in-laws who were visiting from England. During the call, he shared his desire to plant a church in Raleigh, North Carolina and asked us to consider joining him. He asked me to speak to pastor Tito about it, and pray together with Catherine about the opportunity. There was no manipulation in his voice, not even the usual intense and passionate plea I was used to hearing from my bud. It was just a friend, who wanted to check in with a friend, about doing a church plant together.

Catherine got excited as soon as I mentioned it, as did her parents when we talked with them about the invitation. The next morning I spoke to pastor Tito about it and with tears in his eyes and in the most honoring way, he felt peace and blessed me to go for it. Five days later, I chatted with my own parents about it and they were on board, encouraging me all the way. Every person with a place of authority and influence in our lives during that season felt that it was from God for us to move to Raleigh. I was the only one who felt absolutely nothing! This was a strange experience for me. I usually feel, see, pray and dream about important decisions, such as this. This time, my heart felt confirmation, simply because my mothers and fathers believed it would be the best. Catherine had a huge GO in her spirit and her "buy-in", added to all of my fathers' "buy-in"s, gave me the biggest YES I had ever received.

Something had changed in me that was not the result of my efforts to be humble. For the first time in my life, I had received counsel from those I was used to rebelling against and I discovered that God really enjoyed that. I have now been in Raleigh for five years and counting, imitating Duncan and Kate as they imitate Christ. Duncan has taken the time, week in and week out, to share his life with me. Yes, he is far from perfect, but he is perfectly used by God to lead me. Together, we have traveled a journey that has challenged me to the core and I find myself on the shoulders of a giant who, more than anything, wants me to be a giant myself. Or as he likes to say: "An incredible father is someone who not only raises you up as a son, but sees *you* as a great father yourself."

Today, I am convinced, that those who are prepared to surrender their desire for individual gain will experience the joy of sonship in the same measure Jesus did. Don't fear it. Imitating others does not hinder originality, it actually empowers it from the proper platform of permission. It is a sign of maturity that creates the healthy atmosphere for growth. Do not listen to the pride mumbles of "I will only follow Jesus". Leaders worth imitating is what the Bible is all about. Being part of relationships that demands emulation is a Godly and powerful thing. Shortly, you will find yourself living the kind of life that will make others say, "I will imitate you as you imitate Christ."

Us the Fathers

"What are fathers called to? Fathers give. Fathers protect. Fathers bestow. Fathers yearn and long for the good of their children. Fathers delight. Fathers sacrifice. Fathers are jovial and open-handed. Fathers create abundance, and if lean times come they take the leanest portion themselves and create a sense of gratitude and abundance for the rest. Fathers love birthdays and Christmas because it provides them with yet another excuse to give some more to the kids. When fathers say no, as good fathers do from time to time, it is only because they are giving a more subtle gift, one that is a bit more complicated than a cookie.

They must also include among their gifts things like self-control and discipline and work ethic, but they are giving these things, not taking something else away just for the sake of taking." [3]

Regardless of your age, gender, status, race, affiliation or denomination, you have been called to parent the next generation. Heaven sees you as a spiritual parent, for that is part of your God-given formation. In your hands are the tools needed for building. In your pockets are the keys that open doors of opportunity. You have the ability to inspire, equip and support those around you. When you are a *son in the Lord*, you have permission to be a parent in the Kingdom.

Author Floyd McClung describes spiritual fathers and mothers as the ones who "enable others to act. They inspire a common vision and challenge the status quo. They model the way to go and encourage the heart." That's you now, father and mother.

The Invitation and the Challenge

When a person is willing to invest time and energy to make others excel through life and ministry, just as Jesus did with His twelve, their fruit becomes a testimony of the ways of the Kingdom.

As pastor Mike Breen shares in his book *Discipleship Culture* "Perhaps we should take a step back at this point and consider what Jesus was able to accomplish. In less than three years, he was able to disciple a group of men, most of whom no one else would have chosen, and taught them to do and to be like him in such a way that, when released, they would change the course of human history forever. He was able to create a discipleship culture in which there was an appropriate mix of invitation and challenge in the way he related to them." [4]

If we could calculate the hours Jesus spent with His disciples, we would discover that He prioritized time with His guys above everyone else. He empowered them, He shared life with them and He taught them to forgive. He did it all because that is what He saw the Father doing. It was God's pleasure for Peter, James, John, Andrew, Phillip, Thomas, Bartholomew, Matthew, James, Simon, Thaddeus and even Judas to be in partnership with Christ.

Jesus was very comfortable when His spiritual sons did greater things than He did Himself. Christ gave them the authority which He earned by life, death and resurrection. He shared with His disciples the mysteries that left others dumbfounded. To all twelve, Jesus gave power to cast out devils and preach the good news.

If you want to read an action-packed chapter of Scripture, look no further than Luke chapter nine. In this chapter, the twelve disciples are sent out to do miraculous wonders, as they preach the Gospel. Hundreds of people receive the touch of God. They multiply bread and fish for thousands. Peter gets the revelation of Jesus being the Messiah. Three of them go up a mountain and see Jesus transfigured in glory. They fail at delivering a kid from a demonic spirit, but Jesus makes it happen. Then, Jesus goes on to talk about his upcoming death. So the disciples fight about who would be the greatest afterwards. Christ resolutely starts walking down the road to Jerusalem so the Samaritans reject him and His team wants fire to rain down on them. And the chapter finishes with the future cross bearer teaching on the cost of following Him.

On the other hand, Luke chapter 10 is a bit different. It focuses on a peculiar group of people called "the 72 others." The evangelist offers no names and no reference to their gender, race or ages. It is an open canvas for our imagination because any of us could fit into that group. We can picture ourselves there when Jesus says to them: "The harvest is plentiful, but the workers are few. Ask the Lord of the harvest, therefore, to send out workers into his harvest field." Then, He makes them (and us) the answer to that prayer when He gives the order, "Go for I am sending you out." [5]

Off they go, sent in pairs to different towns. As the 36 groups walk, they realize that they are Jesus' first impression, for He is not going with any of them. They were sent ahead to "disappoint" the towns that were waiting to see the Christ. These communities wanted the real-thing, not the misfit couples that would come "pretending."

But Jesus' perspective was a little different. He said, "If they listen to you, they listen to me." And they certainly did! The disciples come back full of joy with reports of demons being cast out (it seems like the demons heard best). In response, Jesus shares with them a vision He had of Satan falling like lightning while they were out on their adventure. Then, according to Luke 10:21-22, Jesus goes nuts!

> "At that time Jesus, *full of joy through the Holy Spirit*, said, 'I praise you, Father, Lord of heaven and earth, because you have hidden these things from the wise and learned, and revealed them to little children. Yes, Father, for this is what you were pleased to do.'"

Those verses conceal the greatest expression of joy in all of Scripture; a happy Jesus, full of laughter in the Spirit, manifesting the pleasure of the joyful Father. The expression, "full of joy" comes from the Greek word *agalliáō*, from *agan*, "much, very" and *hállomai*, "jump, leap". Properly, getting so glad that one jumps in celebration; to exult, boast and remain experientially joyful.[6]

I can picture Luke, the doctor, working on his biography of Christ. His interviews are as serious as his surgeries. He diligently collects all the data necessary to create the longest gospel. His compilation, just like a patient's diagnosis, only considers facts, which have been studied, analyzed and reviewed. Then, he intentionally places the word *agalliáō*, which is not a common or overused expression. Luke does not want to make the Savior look foolish, but he is obliged to give a proper account of what the eyewitnesses saw that day; The Son of God jumping, shouting, spinning and celebrating. What an epic sight!

This is a climatic moment in the leadership of Jesus and a hopeful forecast for you and me. Seventy-two willing followers were able to imitate Christ without sacrificing their personalities, voices and quirks. Because they were willing, *and* because He made them able, on that day the world knew Christ seventy-two different ways.

Up to this point, all the action had been reserved for Jesus and His chosen disciples; the ones who preached, healed and declared the Kingdom message. But, not this time; on that day, it was multiplied times 72. Mothers, brothers, uncles, boys and girls, walked into different towns able to manifest Jesus as if they were Him. Therefore, the Trinity had a prime time moment of celebration. *Agalliáō!*

Jesus, full of the Holy Spirit, praised the Father, as an exuberant prayer accompanied His spinning jumps, "I thank you, Father, Master of heaven and earth, that you hid these things from the know-it-alls and showed them to these innocent newcomers. Yes, Father, it pleased you to do it this way."[7]

You and I are those 72 little children, chosen and loved. We are sent out to do the Father's will as the Son, guided by His Spirit. Christ is fully capable of concluding the mission He set out to do, but He took pleasure in letting us be the ones who "go and made disciples of all the nations." Now we discover the culture of God's Kingdom which starts by coming and ends by going. First, we draw near to God for counsel, and then we get to share His love to the broken. As we approach the Savior with our need, we become ministers of reconciliation for others. By His stripes we are healed, now we lay our hands on the sick. Initially we come to the Father as a *son*, and then we become fathers and mothers to the fatherless generation. As we come to God, we get sent to the world. You are the disciple who becomes a leader, the student who becomes a teacher and the son who becomes a father. And, as you imitate others, you will become worthy of imitation yourself. A true leader is not the one who promotes himself, but the one who finds the greatest joy in promoting others. Take time to teach someone what you know. Don't miss the incredible opportunity to become a father or mother who lives to say, "I want you to do better than me." Join the ranks of Jesus and Peter and Paul; leaders who laid down their lives to make room for others. Don't just be an imitator, become one worth imitating.

Go on the adventure others have already begun and set a new trail of risk and faith.

Independence in the Kingdom is a sign of sickness, not freedom. This is not a Lone Ranger's gospel. This is the story of a family, and in it, parenting and sonship matter. Saturate your time with the joy of duplication. And as you do, you will see Jesus move to the rhythms of *agalliáō!*

STUDY GUIDE: CHAPTER 11
ORIGINAL IMITATION

Carlos explains through the example of Paul and Timothy the concept of imitation; how we become like the spiritual fathers in our lives and in turn therefore more like Jesus.

> *"It's time to open your eyes to the parents around you and become a 'beloved and faithful son in the lord' to one of them."*

Do you have any reservations or fears about imitating a leader as Paul instructs?

Pay it Forward

Who can you invest in as a Father?

Initially we come to the Father as a son and then become fathers and mothers to a fatherless generation. Ask the Holy Spirit to show you if there are people He is asking you to get alongside.

CHAPTER TWELVE

A FATHERED GENERATION

We gain the most when we give.
We learn the most when we teach.
We receive the most when we serve.

— RICK WARREN

The recent past has been filled with great men and women of God that have done most of the work alone. Pastors, evangelists and missionaries who have walked a lonely road where they were expected to perform as ten efficient workers, encapsulated in one super person. We have had too many burnouts as a result, and not enough history shaking revivals. Nowadays, we are moving to a different season in a different rhythm. The hour has come where we honor our fathers, surrender our agendas, and win the world, as a team. Friends and colleagues who will submit themselves to each other, with one goal in mind: to become a

stepping-stone for someone else's greatness. Success for the present men
and women of God requires commitment to the next generations, not
just in words but also in action.

"It is amazing what you can accomplish if you do not care who
gets the credit," is a quote attributed to at least three different American
Presidents. I personally love this citation, because as a pastor surrounded
by anointed, good looking and talented people, I find the need to
remind myself that at least once a week. However, I dare to suggest an
upgrade: "It is amazing what we can accomplish as a team, when we
only care to give God the glory!"

One of the most beautiful things that has happened during my
time in Raleigh is when I've seen our Catch The Fire family expose their
moments of weakness and doubts whilst giving all the kudos to Jesus
for His leadership. We are intentional about calling the Holy Spirit
our Senior Pastor. We work hard, we party harder and we continually
remind ourselves of our absolute dependence on our heavenly Daddy,
and in less than five years we have accomplished more than most
churches have done in twenty. We take no credit. We boast in the
Lord, and we continue to surrender. We try our best to make decisions
together as friends. We fail, we try, we endure and we keep moving
forward. We are far from perfect but we are convinced that He likes
us. A lot!

As we become a fathered generation, we are beginning to
understand that we are all sons and daughters, brothers and sisters,
fathers and mothers, resting in the arms of a really big *Abba*. We stand
with each other during defeat and our commitment is to build a culture
of honor that influences all areas of our ministry. We can then dream
together for our movements and churches whilst we celebrate the

victories of other ministries around us. While orphans fight for their place, we, the sons, share the journey.

In Romans chapter 12, I find an invitation that is extremely enticing. "Love one another with brotherly affection. Outdo one another in showing honor." [1]

If there is competition to be had inside the body of Christ, it should be in the area of honor. You can be intentional about making room for others to be recognized. Take the time to let others know how well they did. Write that email that says, "Thank you, I love you." Beat them to it, outdo one another!

If you are ever inclined to compete in the ministry let it be in being last and serving more. It is in this culture where God feels the most welcomed, for honor is the dialect of the Godhead. It is the recurring language of the Trinity and we are all allowed to join in the fun! Father, Son and Holy Spirit have been eternally competing to honor one another.

It goes like this: The Father declares that every knee shall bow and every tongue will confess that Jesus Christ is Lord. Then Jesus says, "The Father is greater than I." [2] And, while the Holy Spirit commits to only remind us of the things that Jesus already said, Christ replies, "You can mess with Dad, you can mess with me, but there is no forgiveness when you mess with the Holy Spirit." Furthermore, the Spirit chooses to be known as the Spirit of Christ, the Son is willing to be a servant, and the Father is known for honoring all.

What would life look like if honor was the language spoken by all? Can you imagine a church that lives and shares like this, every day? Can you visualize a leadership structure that works intentionally under this culture? Those days *have* arrived, and they began with you and me.

The Language of Heaven

During my last year in Toronto, I was given the opportunity to lead one of the nightly meetings at the Freshwind Youth Conference. With more than five thousand people in front of me, I had a fuzzy feeling on the inside that said, "I've made it!"

I was organizing the ministry time at the end of this massive event. Multiple lines were created to allow people to walk through a "fire tunnel." The madness was glorious as radical youngsters laid on hands and prayed for each other. I was getting the crowd focused on Jesus and expectant in the Holy Spirit. After leading them in what I believed was the greatest prayer they had ever prayed, I came down from the platform and made my way to the exits. As I was about to walk out the main doors, a student from the School of Ministry looked over to me and invited me to join him in the prayer line.

I had never liked Zack and the last thing I wanted to do was finish the night pretending that I did. I acted like I had not seen him as I walked towards the door, waving at people and feeling like a million bucks.

Suddenly, God showed up on the scene. I was given ten seconds to decide whether to go back and honor Zack's request, or to continue walking down the road of pride. After a deep breath and a sense of conviction in my heart, I heard the Father invite me to share a prophetic word.

Zach was the son of missionary parents to Latin America and was always friendly and willing to chat. I know that I had absolutely no reason to dislike him, but I had created silly reasons in my mind to dishonor him. "He tries too hard, His Spanish is terrible, He needs more of our values."

Beyond my irrational judgments, God had a different opinion of him. So, I returned to where Zach was and I began to pray for him one on one. By the third sentence of my uninspired prayer, I began to see Zach differently. I began to see his value, to feel his passion, and to engage with the love that God the Father had for him. Then, I began to speak from that place of revelation. It was like a tsunami wave, a rush of words and blessings that began to land on the shores of his heart and mine. After a long time of sharing God's thoughts for him, we ended up on the floor, receiving from the Holy Spirit and becoming friends from that day forward.

The Bible encourages us "to regard no one from a worldly point of view"[3] but rather to see others only through the eyes of their Creator. Now, whether I have reasons to like someone or not, I intentionally approach them even if I am seeing them from a worldly point of view. Then, I ask Jesus for His thoughts for them. And oh boy does it work!

It is amazing what can happen to relationships when we override our perceptions and base our opinion on God's words of love. I firmly believe that if you have nothing good to say about someone, then you have nothing to say, period. Let's be the kind of people that stop assuming the worst about others and let's make time to hear the opinion of the One who designed them.

Manifest Your True Self

Jesus said, "Love your enemies, and do good, and lend, expecting nothing in return, and your reward will be great, **and you will be**

sons of the Most High, for he is kind to the ungrateful and the evil." [4]
Whenever I read this passage it felt like a contradiction to God's
unconditional love. It seemed to devalue the message of grace and the
good news of adoption. If, in order for me to be a son, I had to "love, do
good, and lend" to those who I consider enemies, then Jesus imposed
a condition to my sonship. How could that be? Did He not love me
when I hated, did evil and acted selfishly?

It was after a careful study of the original text and conversations
with the Holy Spirit, that I began to understand what Jesus actually
meant. "You will be sons of the Most High" became "You will properly
convey your sonship to the Highest Being."

Jesus' request was not for us to earn our place as a son, but rather
to manifest our legitimate sonship and receive our reward. When we
show kindness to the ungrateful, we share in the nature of our Father.
When we love the ones who do evil, we expose the character of Christ.
We are sons because He predestined us for adoption, and we display
that sonship when we love our enemies, forgive our parents, and serve
our neighbors. It is then that we will be straightforward about our
true selves.

Most of the people we would call "enemies" are in that category
because of our inability to see them through the eyes of God. If we
learned to die to the impulse of "my way or the highway" then we
might discover the full expression of our sonship in the Trinity. We
are the children of the greatest Father. It is time to love, do good and
give to others, expecting nothing in return. This is the way of the son
who is a number two, and this is the way of the cross, which we must
all carry. The former German diplomat, Johann Von Goethe, once said,

"Treat people as if they were what they ought to be, and you help them become what they are capable of being."

If we have to manifest God's character to those who do evil, then why would you think the standard would be less for those who are in the family of God?

The original use of the word *submission* in Ephesians 5:21, translates "to get underneath and push up." To walk in the spirit of sonship is to put yourself underneath another's mission, and do all you can to make them successful, knowing that as a son or daughter there is an inheritance that lies ahead. Sonship is about security, significance, identity, patience, basic trust, faithfulness, loyalty, humility, and being others-oriented. The ones who know that they are "somebody" in Christ, are willing like Christ, to become nothing. Then they can empower the ones who are "nothing" to become greater than themselves.

Real power cannot be independently acquired. Influence is given to people who are prepared to come under submission. For no one is successful unless other people want them to be.

I'll challenge you with a series of questions which God regularly uses to challenge me: What if all the prophetic words you have received in your life were given to you so you can steward them for others? What if being called to the nations means that you pay, train and send someone else to go in your place? What if being anointed for the ministry means serving in someone else's up and coming church plant?

Know this, sons and daughters: you have been called to greatness. But! Let that not be your concern anymore; let it be ours as your family and let it be God's. Trust your heavenly Daddy to make room for you and honor your Most High God by making room for others.

Motivated by Love

If we haven't first received and experienced God's love for us, our "obedience" will be legalism, our "love for others" will be tolerance and our "worship" will be forced. The Bible says that, "We love because He first loved us." and you will be hard pressed to find any New Testament invitation to "Love God" where "Loving others" is not immediately following. Jesus increased the scope of that revelation when He took it from just "love others as yourself" to, "Love each other as I have loved you. Greater love has no one than this, to lay down one's life for one's friends." [5]

However, Christianity for some is a way to skip hell. Marriage for others is a way to skip loneliness. The church for a few is the tool to feel included, yet it was never supposed to be about what you can get for yourself, it was always about how much you can give of yourself, for others.

A fathered generation is one that motivates their brothers, fights for their dreams and works as a team, for true fathers and mothers are concerned with legacy. They are not fixated on what they can accomplish for themselves, but on what they are able to leave in the hands of the next generation. They are the church in the original model, "The full number of those who believed were of one heart and soul, and no one said that any of the things that belonged to him was his own, but they had everything in common." [6] Most people look for this kind of community because they expect the community to fill their needs and void, but a healthy community will cause the "selfish me" to fear for his life. By Jesus inviting us to take care of those who can do nothing for us, He is saving us from selfish selves.

Yes, indeed there is a price to pay as you make room for others, but

I guarantee you that the joy of empowering them will connect you with God in a way that few other things can. When you choose fatherhood, you encounter the Father in a whole new way.

I'm continually learning this. My ultimate reward in ministry is seeing the people God has given me, succeed, get empowered and even move ahead of me. My greatest joy is my sons and daughters. It is true in the natural, it is true in the spirit, it is true for God.

The late John Wimber, father of the Vineyard movement in Anaheim California, encouraged us to look behind. He used to say that if we were moving forward, but there was no one on our tracks, we were not leaders; we were simply walking. On the same line, once, at a leadership meeting, I was challenged to think of those who influence me and those who are influenced by me. I was asked to assign a name and a face to the people who I needed to invest in as a son, as a brother and as a father. This exercise allowed me to get a real perspective of my position and my effectiveness as a leader.

Therefore, to make sure you are not simply walking, I invite you to take a moment to look forward and figure out who is ahead of you. Do you know who you follow? Can you name your spiritual parents? Next, take a look beside you, and look for the friends and colleagues who walk the road with you. Are you alone? Do you have brothers and sister joining you in battle?

Thirdly, look behind you, Is anyone following you? Are there sons and daughters on your tracks imitating your journey?

Now that you have an idea where you stand in terms of fatherhood, I'll leave you with a prophetic word delivered by the creator of Microsoft, one of the richest and most successful men in the world, "As we look ahead into the next century, leaders will only be those who empower others." Thanks for the reminder Bill Gates.

A FATHERED GENERATION

"The hour has come where we honour our fathers, surrender our agendas, and win the world, as team, Friends and colleagues who will submit themselves to each other, with one goal in mind: to become a stepping-stone for someone else's greatness."

We are not called to be *lone rangers* but to commit to working together as family. When we do this no one person gets the glory but all the glory goes to God.

Are you a part of a community of believers seeking the Kingdom together?

Carlos poses some questions to help you identify where you are in sharing your walk and leading others:

1. Who is in front of you? Do you know who you follow?
2. Who is beside you? Do you have brothers and sisters joining you in battle?
3. Who is behind you? Is anyone following you? Are there sons and daughters on your tracks imitating your journey?

CHAPTER THIRTEEN

IT'S YOUR TURN!

Light yourself on fire with passion
and people will come from miles to watch you burn.

— JOHN WESLEY

I have never disagreed with God more than I did that night. It was a humid Wednesday evening and I found myself inside one of Puerto Rico's maximum-security prisons again. It was my second visit there and, based on our first gathering, I felt confident that good things were about to happen.

We began to lead the group of orange dressed convicts in a time of worship. We had chosen really good songs to start the evening, but it backfired. The words were new to them, and no one could follow along. After worship, I opened up the sermon with a funny story, but failed again. The story did not relate to them at all so no one laughed. I could feel the tension building as the air got thicker inside the room.

The love I felt the first time I visited was absent now. As I scanned the room, I realized there were a lot of new faces. The crowd was bigger than the first time, but it was also less responsive. Very few people smiled, reacted, or even followed the verses as I shared them. As a breeze of dry air, fear filled my mouth and made my thoughts weak and incoherent.

Once again, just like I was in that high school in front of eighty loud and careless souls, I remembered what I learned from Carol Arnott. "Take a step back into your Father's embrace." The problem was that this time, I could not feel any embrace. I heard no encouragement from the Father. I went through the motions, but I felt alone and disconnected. And that was the moment when God got my attention. Right in the middle of delivering what I thought was my most compelling point, I heard the voice of the Father as a fleeting thought that said, "Tell the ones who have sexually abused their daughters, that I forgive them."

Of course I won't!

My mouth kept moving as I shared the gospel, but my mind went into argument mode. God and I had a serious conflict of theology that needed to be discussed; but not here and not now.

"Wait a minute," I thought, "the devil is trying to trick me!" Thus, I began to bring my thoughts captive to the obedience of Christ and prayed to God that I could focus on the task at hand: Saving the lost.

It didn't work. Regrettably for me, I heard the statement again, but this time it was loud and clear. Many times I have heard that voice, as I am sure you have too. It's a whisper on the inside and it sounds like you and talks like you, but it is way nicer and wiser than you could ever be. Yes, *that* voice.

There was no doubt in my heart. God was speaking to me, but I was so shocked at what He said, that I wanted to believe it was not Him. By the third time He said it, there was no shaking it, so I decided to disobey!

"Father there is no way that I am saying that, I don't think you should forgive people that have sexually abused their daughters, and even if I do say it, no one will respond! You know God, it might cost them their lives!" (Inmates in Puerto Rico are not kind to those that are in prison for sexual abuse to minors.)

I made a compelling point, yet my heart pounded in the knowledge of God's grace which is way more infinite than my limited judgments. And so it was, in the one-second where I thought, "I *know* this is God" my mouth began to say the words that I had been trying to fight off for the last ten minutes.

"Oh yeah, and if you have sexually abused your daughters I want you to know that God the Father forgives you."

Crickets. Silence.

Zero Response.

After the longest five seconds of my life I repeated myself but this time, I was miraculously convicted of what I was saying. The guards who were standing at both ends of the front row looked at me mesmerized. I turned back to look at the friends who had joined me, and they could barely understand what was going on. All eyes were locked on me in the hope that I would move forward and forget what had just happened.

Suddenly, a man sitting two rows to my right fell slowly to his knees and began to say, "*Maria! Maria! Perdóname.*" I could only assume *Maria* was his daughter, and for the sake of those that don't speak Spanish yet, *perdóname* means, "Forgive me." The man on the floor started to scream out loud: "Maria, Maria, forgive me."

There are no words to adequately describe that moment. It felt like grace was an actual substance that could be breathed in and everyone in the room took a deep breath. Two men sitting close to this broken father, came close and extended their hands of support. Shock was still present in the room, but fear had been slowly dissipated.

Straight away, another man to my left broke down and started to pray loudly for forgiveness. Tears began streaming down my face and a message was sent to every heart present on that day: If God is *that* good—that He is willing to forgive *that* kind of a sin—then there is hope for me.

One after another, spontaneously and without much direction, these sons began to pray, kneel, lift their hands and call out to the most forgiving Father there is. I then crossed the invisible line the guards had established between the crowd and me, and I came close to Maria's dad who was still on the floor, begging for forgiveness. I joined the other men, touched his back and felt God's presence in a way that I had never sensed before. I spoke into the microphone with no arguments, jokes or clever revelation. I just kept repeating the words: "He loves you; He forgives you!"

After a time of walking around with the team and ministering individually to our new friends, we began to lead people in prayer. They repeated prayers of forgiveness towards their own fathers for the abuse they had endured at home. We lead them in prayers of self-forgiveness for all the wrong choices that had brought them to imprisonment. Then, we closed the night receiving the Father's embrace by the Spirit of adoption. The same embrace Carol received over and over again whenever she took a step back. The same embrace I had received while disagreeing with God. The same embrace the prodigal son received when He returned to the father's house. The same embrace God the Father wants to give to you now.

I now agree wholeheartedly with a fundamental fact of Scripture; God is a good Father! He is not just a good Father to me, but to all of us broken and hurting little children; all of us who need a great father. We cannot give a higher name to God. The Father, He certainly is.

There is a high probability that you have done things in life that make you feel disqualified from His love. We have all sinned and fallen short. Jesus already paid a price even for the things you will fail at tomorrow. You could finish this book, move on and never think about the Father again, but He will still love you perfectly and consistently. The demand of love that Heaven puts on you today is simple.

You ought to receive the gift that has already been paid for. Then, to walk in sonship towards God, will require you to know the Father that Jesus gave away. Unlike the previous fathers in your life who have either abandoned or rejected you, God's fathering is based on continual acceptance and extravagant grace. God has been a Father for eternity. Let Him be a Father to you everyday.

Love Manifested

"And so we *know and rely* on the love God has for us. God is love. Whoever lives in love lives in God, and God in them. This is how love is made complete among us so that we will have confidence on the day of judgment: **In this world we are like Jesus**. There is no fear in love. But perfect love drives out fear, because fear has to do with punishment. The one who fears is not made perfect in love. We love because he first loved us."[1]

Imagine, the next time you spend a whole weekend at home, your family experiences God's love with every word you speak. Afterwards, you decide to visit a friend in the hospital and in the closeness of your shadow, he gets healed. As you walk inside your office on Monday morning, your co-worker shares the story of his terrible weekend, begins to cry and you become the Father's comfort. Shortly after, you have a meeting with a client that looks depressed, you offer a word of encouragement and He decides not to kill himself. Then, your day ends on a supernatural encounter with God, in which you get to see in the Spirit, all the things He will do through you tomorrow.

If not you, who? If not here, where? If not now, when?

Life is more than what you are aware of. There is sonship to be discovered, and if you are willing to surrender the trinity of "me, myself and I," for the reality of the Father, Son and Holy Spirit, you will live the life that you were destined for.

The Gospel stories were not just written so we would be impressed with Jesus. They are supposed to be a mirror for our daily lives. **In this world we are like Jesus**. It is possible for the supernatural to become routine, the unexpected to become normal. Every miracle Jesus did is available for us and to us. For us as the sick person and for us to heal the sick.

Jesus shared this Godly expectation when He said, "This is to my Father's glory, that you bear **much** fruit, showing yourselves to be my disciples."[2] And, much fruit in the original Greek text means: much fruit!

The advantage for us who believe, is that the pressure is off! "For we are his workmanship, created in Christ Jesus for good works, which God prepared beforehand, *that we should walk in them.*"[3]

God, being the best Father of all, will love us despite our failures, but is also fully expectant of our greatness. This was the life of Christ, who was anointed to preach the good news to the poor, to proclaim freedom for the prisoners, to recover the sight of the blind, to set the oppressed free, and to declare the favorable year of the Lord!

Who are the anointed ones now?

As missionary and founder of Iris Ministries, Heidi Baker has taught us, "It's not complicated. Just love Jesus and the one in front of you." That is all it takes to be fruitful.

The Continual Promise

In the Gospel of John we read a prayer that Jesus prayed out loud, "I do not pray for these alone, but also for those who will believe in Me through their word."[4] The focus of that specific prayer is every single one of us. It gives us insight into an actual moment of intimate connection between the Father and the Son; and its main focus is us! This gospel chapter narrates the events just before the crucifixion.

The beloved disciple shares this deep moment of prayer, as Jesus is about to endure the most painful death in recorded history. Jesus takes no time to share a parable. He is not secretive nor speaks in a prophetic language. The prayer is deep, yet simple; the Son prays for connection. His desire is that we experience the same bond of love He has experienced with His Father since before the foundations of the world. He prays out loud that we would be one with Him and one with each other. This priestly prayer is an invitation to the new covenant of union in relationship, glory manifested and experiential love.

This young carpenter is about to exit the world in the most horrible fashion. His followers will deny Him, His people will reject Him, His enemies will torture Him and He will experience separation from His Father. Still, Jesus finds His motivation in love, and the source of that love is His "Righteous Father." This is His ultimate message. He came to show us the Father, as He explains when He prays: "Righteous Father, though the world does not know you, I know you, and they know that you have sent me. I have *made you known to them, and will continue to make you known* in order that the love you have for me may be in them and that I myself may be in them." [5]

Here is the most exciting promise Jesus leaves for our generation. In His most epic prayer, at the most vulnerable time of His journey, Jesus gives us a guarantee that He will continue to show us who His Father is. This God loves you more in a moment than anyone could in a lifetime. And the promise has no expiration date.

Jesus did a phenomenal job at showing us who the Father is. If we have seen Him, we have seen the Father. When He forgives the sinner, we see the Father. When He feeds the multitudes, we see the Father. When He heals the sick and raises the dead, we see the Father. And, as He promises, He will continue to make the Father known to us.

Jesus is the bodily expression of the Father. They are one for eternity, and when Jesus became one with our sin and depravity, He guaranteed that we could be one with His Father just the same. We are privileged to know and experience God the Father, to exactly the same measure Jesus does. This promise stands for you and your family, in every situation and whenever it is needed.

One Body

"May I speak to Carlos please?" said Mike Malavet, my first spiritual dad, as he cleared his throat on the other side of the phone. It took me five seconds to reply, for it was an unexpected surprise, "It's me Mike! How are you?"

After more than twelve years of staying away I receive one of the most rewarding phone calls ever. This man had discipled me when I was just a baby in Jesus. He led the youth ministry that exposed me to the works of the Spirit. He and his wife were the first ones who prophesied about me being a pastor, but in the span of those twelve years, we had only spoken twice. In the most random Tuesday afternoon in the church office, I picked up the phone. (I have literally picked up the phone four times since working for Catch The Fire Raleigh.)

"The Holy Spirit spoke to me this morning, he said, 'You need to call Carlos and ask his forgiveness.'" Tears streaming down my face, I heard Mike and his wife Cecy tell me how much they missed our friendship and connection. As I held back more tears and listened to them, I knew that I was actually the one who severed the healthy ties we had. In my fervor to serve God and move forward, I had treated them like the past. I made choices without considering them, I moved forward with no regard for the community. I blazed forward, while everything behind me burned.

When I returned home from Toronto I longed to get reconnected with my friends and community but things had changed. People changed. I changed.

We saw each other a few times, but the wrong assumptions and the bitter roots did not allow for our hearts to move on. I closed the door to that relationship and they did the same. But God didn't, He never does.

I hung up the phone after a 20-minute conversation and I felt the embrace of restoration. These people were my family but I treated them like commodities. Even after twelve years these spiritual parents were still teaching me a lesson; forgive, follow the Spirit and never give up on people. The church is a household folks, stop treating it like a garbage dump. It's in the gathering of the broken saints that true community is experienced, and there is hope in the heart of God for unity to be seen in the body of Christ. The oneness that is ours now in the Son and the Father is also manifested in the church family. You can dream of restoration, and you can open your hearts to experience God's love as you reconnect with those who have closed the door shut. If following Jesus is a private venture on your spiritual progress, then church might be optional. But that's not what it is! This journey of sonship requires an outward expression for its legitimacy. It is in the body of Christ where we encounter the greatest expression of His love.

Your Permanent Status

After you finish reading this book, Jesus will continue praying. Whether we are grateful or not, He is continually serving us through intercession. His placement and role, at this very moment, is at the right hand of the Father interceding for us. [6] He is our advocate and He is praying down all spiritual blessing. Yet, the goodness won't stop there, this relationship won't stop when we die.

The one who conquers, I will grant him to sit with me on my throne,
as I also conquered and sat down with my Father on his throne.

— REVELATION 3:21 (ESV)

I always assumed the "right hand of the Father" meant a smaller, yet important throne next to His, but this passage offers a clear and visual explanation. The right hand of the Father is as far as the right hand can be extended, which when we sit down it is usually as far as the right knee. Jesus sat with His Father on His throne and we get to sit with Him on His. The "problem" here is that Jesus' throne is already on top of the Father's throne. Unless your claustrophobia follows you into heaven, we are going to be happily crowded as we all sit on Jesus, who sits on the Father.

God's right knee is your home. It is today and it will be forever. It is available in times of trouble, it is your comfort in times of need, but it is also, your place of acceptance for eternity. You will never cease to belong.

Sons, Fathers, Daughters & Mothers Changing the World

Here we are. We live on the earth as witnesses of the Savior in a world that needs saving. We can manage our tasks from two different perspectives. Either we pray as servants, "Use me God," or as His children ask, "what's the plan Dad?" Sometimes saying things like,

"Use me" implies being manipulated, controlled and given a forced assignment. It is like the puppet master who pulls on all the strings necessary to get his characters to talk, to move and to perform. By now you should know that God is a loving father, not a controlling boss! He wants you working *alongside* Him, not just *for* Him. The plan is to get you to change the world, not to hide from it. His intent is for you to be the head and not the tail; the salt that gives flavor and keeps things from getting rotten; a light upon a hill that reveals His goodness and majesty.

You might ask, "What is God's will for my life?" His will is to love you. Your response is to love Him back. The outworking of both, is to love others. "So also Christ did not exalt himself to be made a high priest, but was appointed by him who said to him, 'You are my Son, today I have begotten you.'" [7] Just as He did with Jesus, the Father will appoint you based on your sonship and His love, not on your qualifications.

Right now, there are teachers and evangelists, millionaires and missionaries, executives and young leaders, board members and janitors, students and professors, doctors and mothers, orphans and sons; all of whom finishing this book are asking, "What's next?"

Well, now it is your turn to write *your* book, get *your* 1.4 million, start revival in *your* local high school, preach forgiveness in *your* local prisons, be part of a team that wins the world for Jesus, and much more! The prodigal Father has not embraced you so He can modify your behavior, but to reveal your identity as a king, friend, lover, servant, bride and son. Start manifesting those value statements. You are allowed to share your story, equipped to love your enemies, and set up to see renewal in your nation. You can stop the sex trade, feed the surrounding poor and adopt babies who need a home. It is for you to reach the most unreached people in this world and to give your life to see "His kingdom come, on earth as it is in heaven."

As the prince of preachers, Charles Spurgeon would say, "Giving is true having."

I charge you to move forward in the calling that God has given you as His child. This is your Father's business and you are your Father's choice. Jesus has empowered you to be an agent of change, a minister of reconciliation and a fire starter in your surroundings.

John Arnott will never be able to preach your sermons. Bill Johnson will not be able to heal your coworkers. Billy Graham is not available to save your family. It is up to you. Not because you have to, but because you get to. This is your inheritance to enjoy.

The choice is simple. Receive the truth that God loves you and that He believes in you or do not, but it's time for you to decide. No more pages to turn. No more words to read. Only the Son Jesus saying to you, "**Very truly** I tell you, whoever believes in me will do the works I have been doing, *and they will do even greater things than these*, because I am going to the Father. And I will do whatever you ask in my name, so that the Father may be glorified in the Son. You may ask me for anything in my name, *and I will do it.*" [8]

You are designed for inheritance. Welcome to your happy sonship. Now go and change the world.

STUDY GUIDE: CHAPTER 13
IT'S YOUR TURN!

Carlos explains the demand of love:

> *"You ought to receive the gift that has already been paid for.*
> *Then, to walk in sonship towards God will require you*
> *to know the Father that Jesus gave away."*

How confident do you feel in freely accepting His continual love and extravagant grace?

Carlos describes what our daily lives could look like when we are walking in sonship.

Do you think this life is for you? If not, why not?

Talk to the Holy Spirit about your doubts; ask him to show you the reality of life with Him. Our oneness with Jesus is reflected in the church, we are called to be united in brotherly love. Paul teaches us that only when we are united in love with one another can we fully know the mysteries of God.

> *"My goal is that they may be encouraged in heart*
> *and united in love, so that they may have the full riches*
> *of complete understanding, in order that they may*
> *know the mystery of God, namely, Christ."*

— COLOSSIANS 2:2

1. Ask the Holy Spirit to show you if there is anyone who you need to restore relationship with, either to ask for forgiveness or to ask to be forgiven?
2. Ask someone to hold you accountable by having the hard conversation and making things right.
3. How will you change the world? Sons and daughters get to help with the family business, the business of seeing the Kingdom come.

This is your mandate:

> *"Very truly I tell you, whoever believes in me will do the works I have been have been doing, and they will do even greater things than these because I am going to the Father. And I will ask whatever you ask in my name, so that the Father may be glorified in the Son. You may ask for anything in my name and I will do it"*
>
> — JOHN 14:12-14

With everything you have learned and begun to experience how will you move forward into the things He has called you to?

EPILOGUE

When I started writing this book I had no idea that every single concept in it would be tested in my life.

Again.

God took me back to the painful question, "whose son are you?" more than once.

He invited me again to trust my fathers. To believe the best. To die to my ambitious self.

I realize that this journey of sonship will last a lifetime. That there will always be orphan tendencies that want to rob us from real authenticity. But blessed are those who give up their masks in order to stay in the light.

Humble. Willing. His.

I warn you in love again, that the main thing that the enemy will tempt you with will be to believe something of yourself that you are not.

But remember, always remember, you are loved for who you are, not for what you do.

You will always be loved perfectly. Even in the midst of your greatest (and most evident) imperfections.

Keep your eyes on Jesus my friend.

And a smile upon your face.

NOTES

INTRODUCTION

1. Galatians 3:26-28 (ESV)

CHAPTER ONE

1. Luke 15:20 (parentheses and emphases added)

2. Genesis 41:42

3. Luke 15:23 (ESV)

4. Steve Roberts paraphrasing from an unknown dictionary source. www.steverobertz.net/writings/tag/parable-of-the-prodigal-son (Retrieved 6 March 2014)

5. Ephesians 1:4-5

6. Acts 17:28

7. John 5:19 (author's paraphrase)

8. Matthew 13:55

CHAPTER TWO

1. Genesis 11:4

2. Mark 1:11 (NKJV)

3. *The Signature of Jesus*, Brennan Manning (p166-7). Sisters 1996

4. Hebrews 2:17

5. *Jesus of Nazareth: From the Baptism in the Jordan to the Transfiguration*, Pope Benedict XVI (p26). Ignatius Press 2008

6. Romans 8:29

7. 1 Corinthians 6:17 (ESV)

8. Mark 9:7

9. Mark 14:35-36

10. John 5:20

11. *The Obedient Master*, Timothy Keller. Dutton Adult 2013

12. Mark 14:35-36

13. Mark 14:39 (ESV)

14. Romans 6:5-8 (ESV)

CHAPTER THREE

1. Author of *The Garbage Generation* and *The Case for Father Customer*

2. *Fathers and Sons*, Frank Pittman. Published in *Psychology Today*, September 1993. www.psychologytoday.com/articles/200910/fathers-and-sons (Retrieved 6 March 2014)

3. *Catch The Fire ILSOM Teaching Notes* (Chapter 7, *The Loving Father* - Part 2). Revised March 2012

4. Matthew 7:11 (ESV)

5. Psalm 27:10 (ESV)

6. Isaiah 66:13

7. Genesis 25:28 (ESV)

8. Genesis 32:24 (author's paraphrase)

9. Genesis 32:27-28

10. Gordon Dalbey. www.abbafather.com/articles/article_hfw.pdf (Retrieved 6 March 2014)

11. John 14:18

12. John 14:21 (ESV)

13. Luke 2:10

CHAPTER FOUR

1. *Sons and Daughters: Spiritual Orphans Finding our Way Home*, Brady Boyd. Zondervan 2012

2. *Anguish of the Abandoned Child*, Charles A. Nelson III, Nathan A. Fox and Charles H. Zeanah, Jr. Published in *Scientific American*, April 2013. www.adoptionpolicy.org/sad0413Nels3pRV.pdf (Retrieved 6 March 2014)

3. 1 Corinthians 2:9-10 (ESV)

4. John 14:6

5. Romans 8:15-17 (ESV)

CHAPTER FIVE

1. Isaiah 14:13 (author's paraphrase)

2. John 8:44-47

3. Rom. 6:16

4. James 4:7

5. Romans 12:2

6. Ephesians 2:4-6 (ESV)

CHAPTER SIX

1. John 6:38-40

2. 1 John 1:8-9

3. John 6:54

4. Colin Urquhart. www.colinurquhart.com/Article/21/In-Christ-Jesus.aspx (Retrieved 6 March 2014)

5. John 17:17-21

6. John 15:3

7. 1 John 2:1-2

8. James 5:16 (ESV)

9. John 1:7

10. Galatians 5:22

11. Jude 1:24 (ESV)

12. Revelation 17:14 (ESV)

CHAPTER SEVEN

1. Joshua 1:1-2 (ESV)

2. Acts 3:26

3. Luke 22:27

4. Mark 10:44-45 (ESV)

5. Mark 10:45 (ESV)

6. Philippians 2:3-8 (*The Message*)

CHAPTER EIGHT

1. 1 Samuel 17:37 (ESV)

2. 1 Samuel 17:55-58 (ESV)

3. Psalm 89:26

4. Psalm 103:13

5. Luke 1:32

6. Psalm 68

7. I Samuel 22:3-4

8. 1 Samuel 26:25

CHAPTER NINE

1. *Hosting the Presence*, Bill Johnson. Destiny Image 2012

2. Luke 2:48

3. Luke 2:49

4. Luke 2:51

5. Luke 2:52

6. John 2:3

7. Exodus 20:12 (ESV)

8. Matthew 13:55

9. Acts 1:14

10. Exodus 20:6

11. Matthew 6:14-15

CHAPTER TEN

1. Romans 8:19 (ESV)

2. 2 Kings 2:15

3. Luke 6:31

CHAPTER ELEVEN

1. 1 Corinthians 4:14-15 (ESV)

2. Philippians 2:20 (ESV)

3. *Father Hunger: Why God Calls Men to Love and Lead Their Families*, Douglas Wilson. Thomas Nelson 2012

4. *Building a Discipling Culture*, Mike Breen & Steve Coclram. Zondervan 2009 (2nd Edition)

5. Luke 10:2-3

6. *HELPS Word Studies.* Helps Ministries Inc 1987

7. Matthew 11:25 (*The Message*)

CHAPTER TWELVE

1. Romans 12:10 (ESV)

2. John 14:28

3. 2 Corinthians 5:16

4. Luke 6:35 (ESV)

5. John 15:12

6. Acts 4:32 (ESV)

CHAPTER THIRTEEN

1. 1 John 4:16-19

2. John 15:8

3. Ephesians 2:10 (ESV - emphasis added)

4. John 17:20 (NKJV)

5. John 17:25-26

6. Romans 8:34

7. Hebrews 5:5 (ESV)

8. John 14:12-1

ACKNOWLEDGMENTS

It's not happy people who are thankful;
it's thankful people who are happy.

So many people have had an impact on my journey that it is unfair to single out just a few, but it must be done.

To my friend and editor Abdel Valenzuela, it's amazing how good you are at everything you do and how well you make these talents available to the people you love. I owe you big time!

To my dear mother Vilma for teaching me how to smile, trust God and to cook rice and beans. To my sisters Beli, Laly, Vane, Kaita and Krystal and to all my nieces and nephews in Puerto Rico. Thank you for your support from a distance; I miss you all every day.

My British mom and dad, who helped with proofreading, babysitting and have always treated me as their favorite son. Love you too dudes.

To the incredible Catch The Fire Books team; Jonathan Puddle, Benjamin Jackson, Jon Long, Marcott Bernarde, Rachel McDonagh and Jo Dunbar ... thank you so much for trusting me.

I also want to pay tribute to our team and staff at Catch The Fire Raleigh. It is incredible to be part of the mission of Jesus alongside some of my favorite people ever!

Thank you mama Kate for believing in my family and my talents (you are truly amazing). Murray and Ash Smith for being incredible servants and available friends. Adam and Anna Walton for manifesting sonship to us, daily and beautifully. Ashlee Brewer for enduring the journey with me and loving my family every step of the way. Mark and Sarah Tillman for going after your album and helping me believe. Amber Brooks for sharing your life, your music and your wine with us. To Caleb Durham, for helping me with ideas, design and encouragement. To Yuki Tanaka and Lianne Batty for helping me with life and schedules and always doing it with willing hearts. To the pastors, staff and interns who are serving in our church community, I thank you for giving me space to write this book. And to Sven, Eli, Noé and Joah; love you four.

A special thank you to Titi Kristen, the best example of Jesus' heart to my family.

Most importantly to my precious wife, Catherine Rachel. The privilege of being with you everyday is not something that I take for granted. I am so grateful for your beauty, your compassion and your growth. There is no way any of this could have ever happened if it wasn't for your love, your prayers and support. You are my inspiration, my hero and my darling girl. Gracias mi Reina, te amo mas que nunca.

I want to finish by celebrating the life of my boys, Carlos Alejandro and Carlos Sebastián. Loving you two is my ultimate favorite thing to do. I'm so proud to be your daddy and you are seriously my best friends in the whole world. I can't wait to read your books, hear your albums, meet your future families and to one day serve under your leadership. I am very excited for your future; but please take it slow—I really enjoy loving you both at home. Becoming your father has made this book a reality, Los amo mis campeones.

ABOUT THE AUTHOR

Carlos is originally from Puerto Rico but met his British darling Catherine while they were both involved in Catch The Fire Toronto. He was interning for pastor John Arnott while she was small group leading at the School of Ministry. After four years of pastoring together in the Caribbean and after three years of leading the Fire Network in Raleigh, and two years as Lead Pastors of Catch The Fire Raleigh, they now serve as Creative Pastors and overseers of Catch The Fire in Latin America. Carlos is also chief editor at HappySonship.com. They have been reaching the city of Raleigh through prophetic evangelism, loving the poor and mentoring students while multiplying radical leaders and having lots of fun! Carlos is a passionate speaker who loves to challenge the "status quo" and Catherine loves to prophesy, give hugs and see the Spirit release His fullness. They are both passionate about revival, their boys Alejandro and Sebastian, their upcoming adoption, and chocolate.

IT BEGINS HERE

The School of Revival is an exciting training program designed to raise up leaders and church planters immersed in the Father's love. We are a non-residential school with no age limit.

So if you are 18 years or older and have a passion to be transformed and see whole Nations changed by the love and power of God then join us on our 2-year adventure here in Raleigh, North Carolina.

International Students who wish to attend the School of Revival may apply for the F-1 Student Visa with the United States Citizen and Immigration Services (USCIS). The School of Revival is fully authorized by the US Government to accept international students and has been awarded the F-1 Academic Institution Student Visa category.

www.schoolofrevival.com

A God who loves you

wants you to experience him

be transformed

and given power

At Catch The Fire, we are passionate about seeing people be transformed by a living God. We have many books that can help you on your journey, but we are also involved in much more.

Why not join us at a conference or seminar this year? Or come on a short-term mission with us? Or have your heart radically changed at a 5-month school. Or just visit one of our churches in many cities around the world.

CONTINUE YOUR JOURNEY AT

catchthefirebooks.com/whatsnext

CATCH THE FIRE®

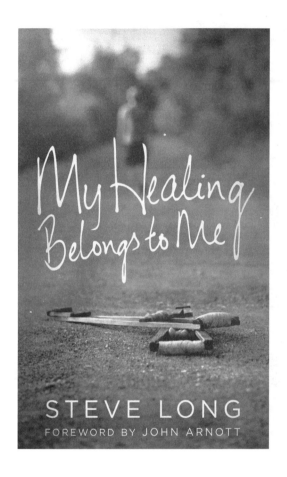
MY HEALING
BELONGS TO ME

STEVE LONG

CONSUMED BY LOVE

DUNCAN SMITH